Too often, when so[me] church, they immedia[tely] it comes. *The church i[s]* misunderstanding of the biblical principals of stewardship. A steward is just a manager of God's resources! In *Generous Life Journey* Gunnar Johnson draws on years of research and hands-on ministry to unpack true, biblical stewardship. What you learn just might change your life!

—DAVE RAMSEY
*NEW YORK TIMES* BEST-SELLING AUTHOR
NATIONALLY SYNDICATED RADIO SHOW HOST

If you're thinking this is just another book about tithing, let me assure you—what God has given Gunnar Johnson to share with those who desire more in their lives and in their churches is greater than anything you've probably been given before. With practical applications, valuable tips, and godly wisdom and insight, Gunnar has written a book that encompasses all aspects of your life and helps you discover what you're supposed to be doing—and all that God has for you. Gunnar says life with God is an adventure, and his encouragement to us is: "Let the adventure begin!"

—JOHN C. MAXWELL
BEST-SELLING AUTHOR, LEADERSHIP EXPERT
FOUNDER, EQUIP INTERNATIONAL

I've had the privilege of walking with Gunnar Johnson on his personal generosity path over the last ten years. His success story is very simple: he listened to God and obeyed. You will be encouraged in your own journey by learning more of his!

—SHARON EPPS
PARTNER, WOMEN DOING WELL

It has been my privilege to consult with and coach leaders from some of the most effective churches in America, and there is no doubt that Gunnar Johnson is truly one of the good guys.

His work at Gateway Church has been a model for so many of us who are working to inspire generosity, stewardship, and giving. I am confident that the wisdom in his new book will help countless Christ-followers find the financial freedom the Lord wants for each of us.

—CHRIS WILLARD
COAUTHOR, *CONTAGIOUS GENEROSITY*
DIRECTOR, GENEROSITY INITIATIVES,
LEADERSHIP NETWORK
GENEROSITY STRATEGIST, GENERIS

I had the privilege of watching Gunnar Johnson develop into one of America's leading stewardship pastors. He speaks with experience and authority. He is a person who walks his talk personally, but more than that, he is able to communicate what he knows in a compelling and transferable way. I recommend this book heartily.

—RON BLUE
FOUNDING DIRECTOR, KINGDOM ADVISORS

Gunnar Johnson's own journey to a generous life qualifies him as a very capable guide! Read the book and put God's principles into action.

—CHUCK BENTLEY
CEO, CROWN FINANCIAL MINISTRIES

Gunnar Johnson teaches us that financial problems are really spiritual problems. The secret of financial freedom is really a "heart issue." This book is biblical, yet practical. It's hard-hitting, yet easy to read as he takes us on his own personal journey from bondage to mammon, toward financial freedom.

—WAYNE HILSDEN
LEAD PASTOR, KING OF KINGS COMMUNITY, JERUSALEM

# *Generous*
# LIFE JOURNEY

## GUNNAR JOHNSON

GATEWAY
CREATE
PUBLISHING

Most CHARISMA HOUSE BOOK GROUP products are available at special quantity discounts for bulk purchase for sales promotions, premiums, fund-raising, and educational needs. For details, write Charisma House Book Group, 600 Rinehart Road, Lake Mary, Florida 32746, or telephone (407) 333-0600.

GENEROUS LIFE JOURNEY by Gunnar Johnson
Published by Gateway Create Publishing
Gateway Create Publishing
700 Blessed Way
Southlake, TX 76092
www.gatewaycreate.com

Cover design by Justin Evans

Visit Gateway Church's Web site at www.gatewaypeople.com.

International Standard Book Number: 978-1-62998-588-6
E-Book ISBN: 978-1-62998-699-9

First edition

16 17 18 19 20 — 987654321
Printed in the United States of America

Gateway Create gratefully acknowledges the partnership of Charisma House in distributing this book.

*I want to dedicate this book to my Lord and Savior Jesus Christ, who demonstrated His love by giving Himself to cover my sins.*

# CONTENTS

# ACKNOWLEDGMENTS

I AM THE PRODUCT of a loving Savior, Christ Jesus, and great family, friends, and mentors.

For your unconditional love as we live this adventure, I would like to thank my wife, Missy, and my kids—Faith, Katelyn, and Elijah. My parents, Curtis Johnson and Melynda Bonner, as well as my in-laws, Steve and Debbie Mathews, have all been a priceless source of wisdom and encouragement.

A special "thank you" goes to my senior pastor, Robert Morris, for teaching me so much about generosity, stewardship, and modeling godly leadership. And also to my Gateway Church oversights: Tom Lane, Todd Lane, and Kevin Grove who have helped me weave stewardship ministry into a growing, local church body.

God has blessed me with some amazing mentors who taught me, encouraged me, and modeled biblical stewardship: Dale Brooks, Sharon Epps, Chuck Missler, Chuck Bentley, Dave Ramsey, Howard Dayton, Ron Blue, Patrick Johnson, Chris Goulard, Dave Briggs, Jerry Schriver, and Dick Towner.

To the most amazing Gateway Church stewardship team who have tirelessly put feet to the ministry vision: Leo Sabo, Kiasi Valentine, James Morris, Chad Sykes, Mashelle James, Texana Matthews, and Yoana Sampayo, as well as our incredible volunteer team.

Thank you to my closest friends and prayer team: Tobey and Marsia Van Wormer, Kyle and Amy Rogers, Braxton and Lisa

Corley, Dustin Parker, Daniel Rowland, Ron Brooks, Martin Day, Mark Mueller, Zach Neese, and Geoff Cohen.

And thank you to those who helped me get my teaching on paper: Henry McLaughlin, my editor, Joyce Freeman, Bobby Williams, Craig Dunnagan and the Create team, and the never-out-of-energy or laughs, my project manager, Marsia Van Wormer.

# FOREWORD

IT MAY BE the oldest concept in the Word of God. It was certainly at the root of Earth's first family's very first assignment. And it was a failure in this area that plunged the world and all humanity into darkness, scarcity, and death.

I'm talking about *stewardship*.

God put Adam and Eve in a place of abundance and gave them instructions to "cultivate and keep" it (Genesis 2:15). That's a stewardship assignment. A loving Father encouraged them to eat freely of every amazing tree in that amazing garden. Any and all—except one. One tree was to be left untouched. Unconsumed.

That, too, was a stewardship assignment. Faithful stewards don't consume for themselves what a generous, holy God says is to be His and His alone.

God's plan always was and still is for us to enjoy abundance through stewardship and generosity. And when Jesus, the Last Adam, came and made right everything the First Adam had messed up, that kind of blessing and joy became possible once more.

Now, as it was back then, the key concept is stewardship.

Cultivation of a lifestyle of generosity is a very personal subject for me. Before my life was completely transformed by an encounter with Jesus Christ, I was chronically selfish, proud, and materialistic. When God's love took hold of me, it turned a very self-centered and self-destructive young man into someone very different.

When, at the age of 19 in a shabby little motel room, I got saved, the first thing I wanted to do was give. I wanted to give to everyone I could. I wanted to bless others and help them know what I had found. Why? Gratitude. I was just unspeakably grateful for the forgiveness, freedom, peace, and purpose I found in God's gift of Jesus.

That was many years ago. As a pastor over the last several decades, I've encountered countless precious couples and individuals who love God and belong to Him—and yet are not experiencing any of the blessing, joy, and peace Jesus died to make available to them. In fact, most Christians in our culture are suffering from the very same financial diseases as those who don't know God.

It's an epidemic in our culture. A 2013 study by a banking organization revealed that 76 percent of America's households are living paycheck-to-paycheck. And a full 50 percent of us have less than a three-month cushion of living expenses in savings. More than 25 percent have no savings at all! An appalling number of people are essentially drowning in debt.

It's one thing for people who do not know God—those who have not been delivered from the enemy's grasp at the cost of Jesus's very blood—to live this way. But for God's redeemed people to do so is a tragedy. An unnecessary tragedy.

That is why teaching people to live blessed lives by following God's principles of faithful stewardship has been a core part of our mission of Gateway Church from its first day of existence. I'm convinced the reason we have been so blessed as a church is that we have endeavored not only to teach these truths, but also to follow them.

We just keep endeavoring to be good stewards with what God gives us, and He just keeps entrusting us with more.

That brings me to the book you now hold in your hands. I believe it is very much a key to a better life for you and your family. A blessed life.

Years ago the elders of Gateway Church recognized that ministering to people in the area of financial freedom and stewardship would require more than just periodic teaching from the pulpit. We saw that people not only needed to understand the spiritual principles and precepts of stewardship, but they also needed practical, specific help in areas such as budgeting, debt elimination strategies, priority settings, and much more.

We established an entire department dedicated to helping our members walk out powerful, practical, and biblical solutions to their financial challenges. And Gunnar Johnson has been instrumental in carrying out and growing this vision from the beginning.

Over the years I've watched Gunnar personally walk hundreds of couples and single parents step-by-step out of the dark financial forests in which they thought they were hopelessly trapped—guiding them into the bright sunshine of financial freedom and blessing. I can't think of any individual better equipped to help you make the same journey to blessing.

I'm excited for you to grasp the truths Gunnar shares on the following pages because I have a powerful passion for seeing God's people walking in all the blessing and kingdom effectiveness that results from a lifestyle of generosity.

Nothing gives me more joy than to see people stepping out and stepping up to this kind of life. Not "giving to get." Giving to honor God. Giving out of gratitude to Jesus. Giving to break the hold of the spirit of Mammon. And being abundantly blessed—not just in their finances but in every area of their lives—as a result.

You're in good hands. My prayer is that you'll open your heart and your mind to the concepts you'll find here. And that as you do, you'll find the courage to embark on the exciting, rewarding journey of living a generous life.

—ROBERT MORRIS
SENIOR AND FOUNDING PASTOR,
GATEWAY CHURCH

# INTRODUCTION

D ID YOU EVER dream of winning the lottery and what you would do with all that money? Pay off your debt? Build your dream house? Pay off your parents' or your in-laws' debts?

Well, I don't play the lottery, but I have to confess, on a few occasions, I have thought about my game plan if I did win.

A few years ago my wife, Missy, asked me a similar question: "If money was no object, what would you do?" That question sent me into several months of prayer to figure it out.

Fast forward about ten years, and, today, I am blessed to be doing my dream job: I pour my life into my home church and connect with other churches—training leaders to lead stewardship ministries and teaching people how to become free both spiritually and with money, and showing them how to live what God created them for from the beginning of time. I get to serve God's people, helping them to make their lives better.

Many mornings I have to pinch myself to see if this is a dream or reality! The desire in my heart is to equip you to maximize your life in God's kingdom. If I am successful in loving and teaching people God's Word about generosity and money, then I have accomplished my calling.

The purpose of this book is to teach you how to be financially free, how to fulfill the plan God has for your life, how to be a blessing to the body of Christ, and how to live a blessed life. This is a simple book explaining what the Bible says about money and how to actually live it.

In each chapter I'm going to lay a firm, biblical foundation for the principles I'll cover. If I can talk you into believing something with just the persuasion of my own words, someone else can talk you out of it. But if you see it for yourself grounded in the Word of God, it will become a conviction.

Acts 17:11 reminds us of the people of Berea, whom, when they heard Paul and Silas, "listened with all the readiness but they searched the scriptures daily to find out whether these things were true." Anytime you hear something taught about money, be like Bereans—go to the Word and check it out!

A lot of junk about finances has been preached, and people in the body of Christ have been hurt and wounded. As a church leader I apologize for that hurt, and I ask for your forgiveness for the way well-intended, but misguided, clergy have taught generosity and finances in the past. Please take a moment to hit the "reset" button on what you've heard about finances.

Let's start with a clean slate.

I want to get you rerooted in the Word in the area of finances. When you see it in the Word, the power of the Holy Spirit will transform your life.

In this book I also provide a practical tool to help you live a life of generosity. It's called the Route 7 Road Map, which I introduce at the end of chapter 3. This road map gives step-by-step instructions to get your finances in order according to the Word of God. At each destination there are substeps to complete before moving on to the next. It's important that you complete each step along the journey before you move forward because they will challenge you to apply the biblical principles we discuss throughout the book.

# Chapter 1
# WHERE FAITH MET FINANCES

'LL PROVE THIS tithing thing doesn't work. I'll tithe my way into bankruptcy. God does *not* work in our finances in this modern day and age."

At the age of twenty-three I was newly returning to my walk with the Lord and thought I knew everything. A friend challenged me to tithe, which led me to wrestle with Malachi 3. The chapter talks about bringing the tithe to the storehouse and watching God open the windows of heaven and pour out blessing. I didn't see the windows of heaven open in my life, but I didn't think tithing would really bring that result. So I set out to prove the Bible, and my friend, wrong.

I began giving God a tenth of my income, but there was no faith in my actions or my attitude. I was putting this tithing thing to the test.

To my surprise, financial and heart changes began to happen. I could see results—they were coming slowly, but they were coming. My wife, Missy, and I began to have just enough, then a little extra, then more and more margin.

Up to that point, my journey to truly surrender everything to God had been a meandering one. I grew up in church. My mom served on the worship team, and my dad was very involved in various church functions. The church we attended was large and growing, so there was always something going on. My parents worked hard to be able to send me to a private

Christian school, so being in church and around Christians was second nature to me.

Then disaster struck. When I was in the eighth grade, my parents divorced. I didn't see it coming, and I didn't handle it well. Over time, my parents had just grown apart.

After that point, my home life became less than stable. When my mom decided to remarry, I moved in with my dad because I didn't like my stepfather-to-be. But I went back and forth between my mom and dad as the mood hit me. Dad had the easier rules, but life with him could be unpredictable.

I became something of a nomad, living from place to place—with Mom, Dad, or friends as the mood hit me. Through it all, I always found a way to land on my feet. I worked at a movie theater at night and mowed lawns during the day. By the time I was fifteen, I owned a cool 1978 Honda 750 motorcycle and a customized 1967 Ford Econoline van. Without much structure in my life, I ran with a rough crowd. Playing high school basketball was all that kept me out of big trouble.

At seventeen, I went back to church for the reason most guys go to church at that age—because that's where all the hot girls went on the weekend. As I sat in the services, the Word of God slowly broke through my tough-guy barrier and attitude, chipping away at the wall around my heart. My brokenness was exposed, and I realized how much I was hurting and how much I needed a Savior. But I also realized something else: God loved me the way I was. My love for adventure was placed there by a God of adventure—Jesus.

During this time of searching for my foundation in Jesus, a coworker at the movie theater challenged me to read Josh McDowell's *Evidence That Demands a Verdict.* I've always been one to question, challenge, and search the Scriptures for answers. God used this intellectual bent to draw me closer to Christ, and I accepted Him as my Savior on October 17, 1993.

After that decision, my life turned around—not all at once, but it changed.

Soon after my salvation experience, one of the elders in the church arranged for me to go back to the Christian academy I had previously attended. I worked jobs before and after my classes and still had time to play basketball for the school, making first team All State and MVP in our division in 1994.

During this time God began to equip me for the call He had placed on my life to be a church pastor someday. I met my future wife, Missy, in high school. Her family noticed I was still bouncing from house to house and took me in, under strict guidelines. Her father, Steve, a strong Christian with a passion for the Lord and to witness to others, taught me the drywall business. But more importantly he taught me how to walk with the Lord and be a Christian businessman who was full of integrity.

In 1994 I moved with them to Florida and worked in the family drywall business. Steve was known to be a hard worker, and he put me through the paces. This included a stretch of nine months working from sun up to sun down in hot South Florida without a day off.

I suspect it was an extreme test for me. He was trying to drive me off. Or at least he was testing the sincerity of my love for his daughter.

Missy and I married in 1996 and moved back to Fort Worth. Then, in 1998, we purchased a carpet cleaning franchise. We were the youngest owners for this particular brand in the United States, and we soon began making money—a *lot* of money for a young couple.

We spent a great deal of what we made because we weren't ready for success. At twenty-three years old, I hadn't learned how to handle money wisely. So if we wanted something, we bought it without considering the consequences.

We began going to church less frequently, as our hearts were pulled away from God by the money and what it could get us. With our priorities out of order and without a good financial plan, we weren't prepared when difficult times hit—and hit they did. And then they grew worse.

## THE INTERSECTION OF FAITH AND FINANCES

God has interesting ways of getting our attention. One spring, our church held a twelve-week Bible study on finances. I asked myself, "What could the Bible possibly have to say about business and money management?" I thought it was a joke or a trick to get me to give more money.

I was wrong. The class written by Howard Dayton and Crown Financial Ministries quickly opened my eyes, and I saw for the first time the wisdom of the Bible in the area of finance.

That study brought Missy and me to the intersection of faith and finances. We will all come to this intersection at some time in our lives. How we negotiate it will go a long way to determining our success in our walk with God and in life.

It was during this season that my friend challenged me to tithe. I wasn't expecting it, but at the end of that twelve-week study, I realized I didn't have a financial problem. I had a spiritual problem that blocked me from experiencing all God had for me.

When I was growing up, my family didn't have much. Yet at my Christian school, I was surrounded by affluent kids. From a young age, I vowed to make a lot of money and be successful, and I was determined to achieve success and significance on my own. But years later, even as I was achieving those goals, I was hurting.

I realized I was pursuing my ambitions instead of God. Tired of what my efforts alone had produced in my life, I surrendered to the Lord. I prayed, "Lord, I've had enough. I'm tired of fighting this. I'm tired of this unhealthiness in my life, and I'll do whatever You call me to do."

Almost as soon as I finished praying, I heard the Lord say, "Sell your business."

I was shocked, and I didn't want to sell the business. Yet the Lord showed me that it had become an idol. And when I shared with Missy what the Lord told me, she was open to doing whatever God had told me, which, considering Missy's type A personality, I took as confirmation that this is what we should do. So Missy and I obeyed, and the business sold within three weeks.

During this time, Missy and I had made the decision to live and run our business by faith. Then, shortly after we had our first child, a daughter we named Faith to match our decision, we opted to move back to Florida, where Missy's parents operated a construction business. We, too, started a construction business under God's clear instruction to do it without any debt, and we determined to apply biblical principles to everything we did.

Slowly, we started to get out of the debt we'd brought with us from Fort Worth. I believe this is because we chose to be givers and to manage our finances according to biblical principles of stewardship. We were eking by, month-to-month, customer-to-customer, and God provided. Sometimes it seemed like it was at the last second, but He always provided. Because of our obedience and God's faithfulness, the small drywall company grew, and we paid off $88,000 of personal debt as we built the business debt-free.

The calling to pastor that I received at seventeen was renewed. I had run from that calling and focused on achieving success *my* way. When I gave my life back to the Lord, I knew I was called to be a pastor who taught on money, and I knew

I was called specifically to serve in Southlake, Texas, which didn't make sense at the time since Southlake was just a rural community. But God knew what He had planned for that area, and what He told me came to pass many years later. After meeting God at the intersection of faith and finances, I accepted His call to ministry. And in His excellent timing all the right doors opened.

After a few years of diligently studying Larry Burkett's books, listening to Dave Ramsey on the radio, and going through Crown Ministries training, I began teaching stewardship classes in whatever church would have me. This brought me into closer contact with Crown Ministries. I called one day and told them I needed a box of brochures because I was going to start a stewardship ministry in every church in South Florida.

Their Florida state representative, Tommy Beck, quickly contacted me and took me under his wing, training and mentoring me. He reined in my passion and exuberance, and showed me how to focus them in order to bring greater glory to God and more good to His people. I was trained to be a financial counselor and small group leader, and eventually served on staff at Crown Ministries as director for the area of southwest Florida from Naples to Sarasota, funding myself through my drywall company.

In the meantime, God continued to prepare Missy and me for full-time ministry. I plugged into the Word with my usual *all-in* enthusiasm. I wanted to know every chapter and every verse in the Bible. My work was such that I could listen to audio Bibles and Bible commentaries. I was putting in so many hours at work I frequently listened to the entire Bible in a week! I listened to Calvary Chapel expositional commentaries to go deeper into God's Word. One of my favorite teachers was former Calvary Chapel Costa Mesa pastor Chuck Missler, who later founded Koinonia House ministry. I had a series he taught where he devoted one hour to explaining every chapter in each book of the Bible. With my headphones on, I would log more than seventy hours per week as my mind and spirit soaked in God's Word.

During this season, the Lord was also preparing Missy and me to minister beyond the area of finances. We taught young married classes at church and watched the groups grow until we had to split them into smaller groups. We were learning how to minister to different kinds of people, developing our skills to be more effective for Him.

The next surprising step in my calling came when the church I grew up in back in Texas—The Hills Church—called and asked me to be their full-time stewardship minister. We agreed, and once again God used my position to help me grow into new areas of ministry. I learned how to lead and train volunteers. And after completing a ministry development plan under the supervision of the church's experienced ministry staff, I was ordained to be a pastor.

Then one day while I was in prayer, God told me to get ready to leave The Hills Church. I didn't want to go. I loved my church family and envisioned us staying there until Jesus came. But Missy and I prayed through our unwillingness to leave and reluctantly determined to go whenever God gave the word.

A few months later, I received a call from Gateway Church, which was located twenty miles away in Southlake, Texas. They wanted to start a stewardship ministry and asked me to help. We began to meet, and I gave them material and helped them develop a plan to build a comprehensive stewardship ministry.

Two months later, they called back. They liked the plan, but after praying about it, they felt I should join the staff and lead a stewardship department. I was not expecting this and wasn't sure I wanted to do it. The decision was one of the hardest I've ever had to make. When Missy and I both knew

God was calling me to Gateway, we stepped out in obedience. Due to godly leadership at both churches, the transition went smoothly.

With the help of the full pastoral staff, Gateway has built a growing and comprehensive stewardship ministry. The ministry seeks to serve four groups of people in the area of finances:

- The Struggling—those do not make ends meet

- The Stable—those who are one paycheck from disaster

- The Solid—those who are doing well financially; they aren't wealthy but they have more money than month

- The Surplussed—those with wealth and a high capacity to build more

God's Word equips us to be wise stewards by helping us get out of debt and change our lifestyles. When we make bad decisions, it's usually because we haven't sought God's counsel. I've found that many of my bad decisions were ones I didn't pray about and wasn't willing to discuss with others to get their counsel.

The keys to financial stewardship that I've found, and that I will share in this book, include knowing where your money is coming from and where it's going, and making financial decisions based on a clear spending plan and wise counsel.

Several years ago I was called into a lunch meeting with our senior pastor, Robert Morris, and two other members of the senior pastoral staff. He commissioned me to be a stewardship evangelist and released me to build a national and international stewardship ministry as I had for Gateway Church. *I thought I was going to be fired.* But Pastor Robert didn't fire me, he only encouraged my apostolic calling.

With Gateway as our platform, Missy and I have taught the generosity and stewardship principles in this book to churches across the United States, and as far as Israel and Europe as the Lord has opened doors for this message to spread. We are continually amazed at all God has done.

Needless to say, I didn't tithe my way into bankruptcy. Instead, I have been on an incredible adventure with Jesus as I have learned biblical principles for managing our finances. In this book I will share these principles and practical ways to apply them, so you can also walk in all the blessings God has for you. Let the adventure begin!

# Chapter 2
# LIVING A BLESSED LIFE

THE LIFE MESSAGE of my senior pastor, Robert Morris, is "the blessed life." This message has changed my life and the lives of thousands of others. Having a blessed life can mean different things to different people, so let me explain both what it is and what it isn't.

First, let me tell you what it is not. The blessed life is not a strategy to get rich. It is not a formula for a challenge-free life. And it is not a health-and-wealth prosperity message. You can have a blessed life at any income level.

The blessed life is all about joining God on the crazy adventure He has planned for each of us. As Pastor Robert puts it, living the blessed life means you have the supernatural power of God working for you. The days of a blessed person are filled with divine "coincidences" and heavenly meaning.

Finances are part of living the blessed life, but it's about more than finances. Money is simply a tool in the Christian's toolbox. Living the blessed life has three essential elements:

- Lordship
- Stewardship (or management)
- Generosity

Let's look at each one more closely.

## LORDSHIP

Lordship is the cornerstone of living the blessed life. We are to honor God *with* everything and *in* everything. He calls us to live generously and strategically. When we do this, it makes room for Him to pour blessings into our lives. He is waiting for us to surrender to His Lordship so we can live the blessed life He has planned for us.

God, who loves us, has created us all for a mission in this life. Walking in surrender to the Lordship of our Savior Jesus Christ is the only way to begin the blessed life journey.

The blessed life is not a prosperity theology. It is the reality of what Scripture says about being active in God's kingdom. Prosperity theology is all about following God to get something for ourselves. It is a greedy, give-to-get philosophy. This is not what I teach. I teach a give-to-give and live-for-Christ's-advancement philosophy.

In His Word, God has given us everything we need to live a blessed life and accomplish all He asks us to do. Making those biblical principles work takes application, not just intellectual assent. When we apply God's Word, we build our lives on the solid foundation of Jesus Himself. As we move through this study, you will be encouraged to not only hear the Lord but to also do what He says. That is what it means to make Him Lord.

## STEWARDSHIP

From the beginning God created and called us to be stewards. In Genesis mankind was given dominion over the world and was commanded to replenish the earth and to take care of it. We will go into this in more depth in the next chapter. For now, suffice it to say that we are still called to be stewards. Stewardship simply means management. We have been given the responsibility of managing the earth God created as well as our time, talents, influence, and resources.

The amount of money or time we have isn't what matters. What matters is what's in our hearts and what we are letting God do in our lives. God is looking for stewards who are faithful, people who will diligently and wisely manage the time, talent, and money God gives. I believe God is preparing some to manage millions, billions, and even trillions of dollars for His kingdom.

## GENEROSITY

God does not leave us wondering how to be good stewards. Scripture is timeless and written for all generations. God is not surprised by life as we experience it in this modern age, and He still calls us to a life of generosity.

First Timothy 6:17–19 is one of my favorite foundational stewardship passages. These are the verses God used to call me into ministry and the ones He takes me to when I ask Him how I should be using the resources He has given me.

In this passage, the Apostle Paul is writing to Timothy, a young pastor of the church of Ephesus. This city was a major seaport and economic center of the day. For us, the equivalent would be Boston, Houston, or Los Angeles. So in 1 Timothy 6, Paul is giving the pastor of this growing metropolitan church a short lesson on what to teach people who have resources.

> Command those who are rich in this world that they not be conceited, nor trust in uncertain riches, but in the living God, who richly gives us all things to enjoy. Command that they do good, that they be rich in good works, generous, willing to share, and laying up in store for themselves a good foundation for the coming age, so that they may take hold of eternal life.
> —1 TIMOTHY 6:17–19, MEV

This passage tells us that rich people's hope should be in God, not money. That's a good word for rich people, right? By the way, do you consider yourself rich? You might be surprised that, according to globalrichlist.com, if you earn forty-seven thousand dollars per year, you are in the top .37 percent richest people in the world by income. That means 99.63 percent of the world lives on less than what you make!

You're richer than you may think.

The reality of life is we can never have enough money to be secure or satisfied, or to feel significant. Those needs are spiritual and are met only through our walk with God.

The blessed life does not rise or fall on our level of wealth, but within our relationship with Christ, who calls us to "be rich in good works, generous, willing to share."

I used to think the car I drove and where I lived gave me personal value. Most of our culture has bought into that lie. This materialistic thinking is dangerous and spiritually destructive. Our value has nothing to do with what we drive, wear, or own.

Please don't misunderstand me. There isn't anything wrong with having wealth and buying nice things. Our wealth simply needs to be carefully stewarded. As you live the blessed life, chances are high that you will have extra money to steward. After all, the Bible tells us if we sow we will also reap. That principle applies to love, friendship, kindness, and much more. But it also applies to finances.

God gives us stuff to enjoy, and we shouldn't feel guilty about it. But we should watch for the opportunities He brings our way to be generous. Let's embrace the responsibility God has given us to make a difference in this world.

Part of the responsibility of receiving God's resources is to live within certain margins so we can be generous. What are those margins? There is no magic number or percentage. Life would be easier if God actually gave us a specific amount to devote to living expenses, cars, clothes, charitable giving (out-side of the tithe), and so on, but He didn't. We all have to hear His voice for our specific calling. Through the material in this study, I hope to help you learn to hear His voice, then deter-mine the best amounts for you.

Before I close this chapter, I want to draw your attention to one other statement in 1 Timothy 6. Verse 19 tells us we have a short opportunity to make eternal investments. Life is short—and moving fast! *Carpe diem*—seize the day. We need to make the most of every opportunity to learn, grow, and develop.

Jesus taught that generosity produces treasure in heaven. We will touch on this in more detail in upcoming chapters, but right now pause and consider this thought: Do you live a life in which the supernatural power of God is working for you, where your days are filled with divine "coincidences" and heavenly meaning? If not, why not? Don't you want to?

I do, and I can tell you from experience that it is an awe-some adventure. Join me in the next chapter, and we will sit down and dig deeper into a fundamental aspect of living the blessed life—understanding what it means to be a steward.

# Chapter 3
# FIVE STEWARDSHIP PRINCIPLES

I N MY EXPERIENCE counseling thousands of people and training hundreds of church leaders, I've discovered five stewardship principles everyone needs to understand if they want to live the blessed life. If you and I had just thirty minutes to sit down for a cup of coffee and talk about biblical stewardship, these are the five principles I would share, from one steward to another.

## WE ARE ALL CREATED TO BE STEWARDS

Who are we? Our identity is the most important, most impactful discovery we make in life. To uncover who we are, we have to go back to the beginning.

There is a principle in Bible study called the law of first mention. That means the first place a subject or topic is mentioned in Scripture carries greater weight because it lays the foundation for understanding that concept throughout God's Word. Our role as stewards must be pretty important to God because that is one of the first ways He describes us. In Genesis 1, the word *dominion* is used to explain that we have sovereignty over the earth; that means we are made to be stewards.

> In the beginning God created the heavens and the earth.... Then God said, "Let us make man in our image, after our likeness, and let them have dominion over the fish of the sea, and over the birds of the air, and over the

livestock, and over all the earth, and over every creeping thing that creeps on the earth."

—GENESIS 1:1, 26, MEV

That would include the bugs that creep in my garage! God created us—do not let that slip by you. God created all of us, and He created us to be stewards. Our job is to manage whatever God sets before us to the best of our ability. When I first understood this truth, it changed the way I thought about everything. Understanding stewardship is life-changing.

Stewardship has kind of lost its meaning in the last few years, so I want to go back to its powerful biblical beginnings to explain this wonderful concept. Stewardship is not a fundraising campaign. It's not just about money and giving.

Stewardship is something we do with everything within us and around us. I am a steward of my family, my church, my house and cars, the money entrusted to me, my friendships and influence just to name a few.

When that biblical revelation sinks in, it will change the way you view everything. One time I bought a two-year-old, new-looking, fully loaded SUV. After dinner out one night, as my wife and I walked to the car, I noticed someone had keyed the side of our truck. I was really mad. But the edge of the anger wore off as I allowed the Lord to help me process the situation. I asked why this had happened, because I had worked really hard to buy that truck. God said to me, "*I gave you the ability to buy that truck, and it really is Mine; you only manage it.*"

Honestly, this took some time to sink in, but I never fixed the truck because it served as a constant reminder to not get too attached to things, as if I owned them, but to hold on to them loosely, because I am simply a manager. If the Lord were to ask me to give something away or do something for Him, I need to be willing to do it in a heartbeat, because the item is really His anyway. I'm the steward.

## WE HAVE A MISSION BUT IT'S BROKEN

God created everything. Then He created us with a purpose—
to take care of His creation (Gen. 1:26). But this mission was
broken by sin (Gen. 3).

Ever since sin entered the world through Adam, we have
been searching for success, significance, and meaning in this
life. Paul says it this way:

> For we are His workmanship, created in Christ Jesus for
> good works, which God prepared beforehand that we
> should walk in them.
> —EPHESIANS 2:10, MEV

This was lost to us in Adam's sin. Sin is an immoral act or
transgression against God's divine law, and we have all sinned.
All sin requires a payment before a holy God, and that payment is death. Though Jesus was without sin, He became the
needed payment for our sin. As God in the flesh, Jesus came
to earth, lived a sinless life, and fulfilled thousands of years of
extremely specific prophecy. Then Jesus paid for our sin when
He died on the cross. And by accepting His payment for our
sin through faith, we can be made whole before God.

No matter how good we are, we do not have the ability
to live sinless lives or do for ourselves what Jesus did for us.
Jesus is the only key to fullness in life. Why do I cover this in
a book on finances? Because what many people are looking
for is something only Christ can bring. They use money and
stuff to try to fill this void, but possessions can never suffice
because they are not designed to satisfy us.

Sin destroys our ability to enjoy the gifts God gives us. It
marks us with insecurity, anxiety, and hopelessness. It creates
in us a desire to get rich and build our own kingdom. But the
Bible says, "No one can serve two masters. For either he will

hate the one and love the other, or else he will hold to the one and despise the other" (Matt. 6:24, MEV). We can't serve God and money. According to Jesus, it is just not possible.

Until we decide we're going to follow God at all costs, we won't find real contentment. First Timothy 6:6 says, "But godliness with contentment is great gain" (MEV).

When we are secure in our salvation (and many Christians aren't), we will be able to relax and not feel compelled to chase after stuff. The materialism breaks off, and God can begin to bless us. As He sees us being faithful in the small things, He will begin to give us the true riches of souls to manage.

Understanding sin and the fact that it broke our original mission changes everything. It brings a transformation of our hearts.

I'm spending time on this because I'm a pastor, and I love you. I want you to fully understand what salvation means. I don't want to spend eternity looking across the gulf at people in hell who sat under my teaching but never understood Christ's payment for their sin.

When you wrestle with the question, "Am I saved?" and come to a full understanding of what it means to make Jesus Lord of your life, you will find it a lot easier to be a good steward because there's no resistance anymore.

Matthew 13:22 is our challenge in this modern age:

> He also who received seed among the thorns is he who hears the word, but the cares of this world and the deceitfulness of riches choke the word, and he becomes unfruitful.
>
> —MEV

We can easily fall into this category. We hear the Word but let the cares of this world choke it out. One of my goals is to make sure you don't fall into this trap.

## Jesus Is Our Reconciler

Have you ever lied, looked lustfully at someone not your spouse, or even created an idea of who God is that is not scripturally accurate? If you answered yes to any of these questions, then you have a need for Jesus. All it takes is one sin to spend eternity in hell. But I have great news. Jesus is our reconciler! His sacrifice on the cross brought us back into right relationship with our Father God. He is:

- The foretold Messiah of Israel

- Our Redeemer

- The Designer and Orchestrator of our gifts

- Creator of heaven and earth

- Our Intercessor before God

- The Designer of our heavenly destiny

- The coming Ruler who will judge the world

Christ redeemed us from the curse of the law, and on the Day of Judgment our case will be dismissed due to a lack of evidence if we have accepted Him as our Savior by acknowledging that He paid the debt of our sin.

By the way, did you know there are two ways to get to heaven? (OK, right now your heresy sensors should be going off and you should be saying, "What is he talking about?") The first way is to never have a bad thought, never tell a lie, never lose your temper, and never sin your whole life. The second way is the path we are all on, which is to accept Christ's payment for our sin and rely on what He did, not on what we can do. There is no number of good deeds that can overcome even one of our sins.

If you haven't accepted the gift of salvation—Jesus's payment of your sin through His death on the cross—then repent and turn to Jesus. You can do this by praying this simple prayer between you and God: "Father, I am a sinner, and I need Your forgiveness for my sins. Please forgive me as I accept the payment Jesus Christ made for my sin. I accept Him as my Lord and Savior."

Yes, it really is that easy. God has made it that simple because of His love for you! Now read John 3:16–17.

> For God so loved the world that He gave His only begotten Son, that whoever believes in Him should not perish, but have eternal life. For God did not send His Son into the world to condemn the world, but that the world through Him might be saved.
>
> —MEV

Even if you are a Christian already, this passage should bring a big smile to your face! Your sin debt is paid in full simply because God loves you.

Now that we understand that Jesus is our reconciler, let's get to the mission ahead of us in life. What is next? Good question. Let's look at Luke 19:11.

> As they heard these things, He continued and told them a parable, because He was near Jerusalem and because they thought the kingdom of God would immediately appear.
>
> —MEV

This verse takes place as Jesus was approaching Jerusalem on Palm Sunday. There was a huge crowd and a festive atmosphere. Many of Jesus's disciples and followers expected Him to waltz into Jerusalem, overthrow the Roman government, and set up His own kingdom. In fact, some were arguing over who was going to be the greatest in the new kingdom and who would get to sit at His right hand.

They didn't quite understand what was going on and what Jesus was doing. Then Jesus told them this story, hoping they would catch its meaning.

> He said, "A man of noble birth went to a distant country to have himself appointed king and then to return. So he called ten of his servants and gave them ten minas. 'Put this money to work,' he said, 'until I come back.' But his subjects hated him and sent a delegation after him to say, 'We don't want this man to be our king.'
>
> "He was made king, however, and returned home. Then he sent for the servants to whom he had given the money, in order to find out what they had gained with it. The first one came and said, 'Sir, your mina has earned ten more.' 'Well done, my good servant!' his master replied. 'Because you have been trustworthy in a very small matter, take charge of ten cities.'
>
> "The second came and said, 'Sir, your mina has earned five more.' His master answered, 'You take charge of five cities.'
>
> "Then another servant came and said, 'Sir, here is your mina. I have kept it laid away in a piece of cloth. I was afraid of you, because you are a hard man. You take out what you did not put in and reap what you did not sow.' His master replied, 'I will judge you by your own words, you wicked servant! You knew, did you, that I am a hard man, taking out what I did not put in, and reaping what I did not sow? Why then didn't you put my money on deposit, so that when I came back, I could have collected it with interest?' Then he said to those standing by, 'Take his mina away from him and give it to the one who has ten minas.' 'Sir,' they said, 'he already has ten!' He replied, 'I tell you that to everyone who has, more

will be given, but as for the one who has nothing, even
what they have will be taken away. But those enemies of
mine who did not want me to be king over them—bring
them here and kill them in front of me'"
                                            —LUKE 19:12–27

In this passage from Luke 19, we see four groups the world
can be divided into:

- Those who reject Jesus (vv. 12–14)

- Those who get a tenfold return (vv. 15–17)

- Those who get a fivefold return (vv. 18–19)

- Those who just give back what they were given
  (vv. 20–27)

We serve a King who has gone off to a foreign land to claim
a country, and He'll be back someday. We're in that time frame
of waiting for His return. Everything we do in Christ's name
is rewarded, and we have the opportunity to receive a tenfold
return or a fivefold return. We can experience a great reward
in heaven by helping people come to know Christ, giving generously to help advance His kingdom, or sharing God's love
in many other ways. Or we can just give back what He's given
us—"Hi, Lord. I'm here. I made it. Don't have a lot to show for
it, but I made it." The choice is entirely ours. I will discuss this
topic in detail in chapter 9.

## GOD'S WORD EQUIPS US TO BE STEWARDS

The Bible is the best book you can study on finances. There
are more than two thousand passages on money, and seventeen of the thirty-eight parables Jesus taught are about money.
To not have an understanding of what God's Word says about

money is a significant disadvantage in our walk with Christ and in life!

You can pick up almost any non-Christian book on finances and find a biblical root or foundation for the author's ideas. Many books on financial management espouse charitable giving and being generous with our resources. They tell people to develop multiple streams of income (Eccles. 11:6), to avoid cosigning (Prov. 22:26–27), and to get and stay out of debt (Rom. 13:8). All of these concepts can be traced back to God's Word.

Scripture has a lot to say about money, but it's critical that we not only understand the theology about money but also the practical application. Any asset left unmanaged becomes a liability. That's why my goal in this book is to equip you to take the principles from God's Word and apply them to your finances.

Recently I was in Israel teaching on biblical stewardship. I was having a good time sharing the financial principles found in Scripture, but the Israeli people are a little different from most American audiences I've spoken to. They push back a lot and challenge what you're saying. It's part of their culture. I enjoyed the challenge immensely.

One gentleman said to me, "These are Western culture ideas that won't work here in Israel."

My response was, "These verses were written to Israelis several thousand years ago in the land you live in today. These are not Western principles. They were written to your people in your land in a much more oppressed time than you live in today. These biblical ideas are timeless and have no region. All it's going to take for these ideas to work for you is for you to step out and walk by faith."

It was like a cloud lifted out of the room as he grasped the concept that God's Word prepares us in this day and age to be stewards. What I told him is as true for you as it was for him. The Bible is relevant to every area of our lives, including our finances.

## WE HAVE ONE LIFETIME TO MAKE AN ETERNAL DIFFERENCE

According to World Health Organization statistics from 2012, there are roughly 1.8 deaths every second, 108 every minute, 6,481 every hour, 155,556 every day, 4.6 million every month, and 56 million every year![1] Not a happy thought.

And I can guarantee you one thing—just about all of those people who died were surprised when it actually happened. I see this when I visit hospitals and counsel terminally ill people. No matter how much warning they had, it is still a surprise. Death is like a period in the middle of a sentence.

God wired us for eternity. We naturally think we will live forever. Unfortunately, our broken mission is the reason for the brevity of life, but we don't think about it in those terms. I'm not trying to scare anyone, but I do want you to grasp the fact that our lives on earth are temporary. We have a limited amount of time to live out our calling.

If time is short, the last thing we should want is to miss our calling. There are several ways we do this. The most critical way to miss our calling is to not accept Christ as our Lord and Savior. The Apostle Paul wrote that of all the things he had accomplished in life, nothing was more important that knowing Christ (Phil. 3:5–8).

Jesus Himself said the greatest commandment was to love the Lord with all our hearts, mind, and strength, and then to love our neighbors as ourselves. Nothing we could desire or pursue in life is more valuable than knowing Jesus. And here's the kicker: when we seek God's kingdom and righteousness first, God will provide all the things we need and even things we just want (Matt. 6:33). How sad it is for those who spend their lives running the wrong race, building the wrong kingdom, or pouring themselves into themselves or their own self-existence or into something that doesn't matter.

We can also miss the calling on our lives by getting so wrapped up in greed that we never have enough and our focus is always on getting more. A third way is to fall into analysis paralysis. We never quite figure out what God is calling us to do because we constantly question and analyze. We look for another sign and then another, and we end up not moving at all. God can only guide a moving ship. If you've ever ridden a jet ski, you'll know that you can't steer it until you hit the gas.

My first service as a volunteer in church was watching babies in the children's ministry. I moved on to making announcements at the beginning of Sunday school class. Then I was tricked, due to my terror of public speaking, into teaching half of the Sunday school lesson in the young married couples' class. The next thing I knew, I was teaching the entire hour-long lesson.

God used that experience to build my confidence, and now I'm leading a church stewardship movement all over the country and in Europe and Israel.

Each step in this journey was terrifying, yet I kept pressing forward because I knew God had given me a word, and each step of faith I took pushed me forward to the fulfillment of His word.

To fulfill your calling, you will need to determine your gifts. In chapter 8 we will talk about life stewardship, and you'll learn how to discover your gift set. You'll learn how to assess your gifts to determine what purpose God created you for. We'll walk through a process that will help you figure out how to move in the direction of your gifts to use your life to make a difference.

Part of walking in your calling is to focus on your strengths, not your weaknesses. Weaknesses are hard to improve. We will be more successful when we build on our strengths and on the gifts God has given us.

The opportunity to make an eternal difference only happens once. Remember the parable in Luke 19 and get aggressive about investing your life to receiving a maximum return.

# The Route 7 Road Map

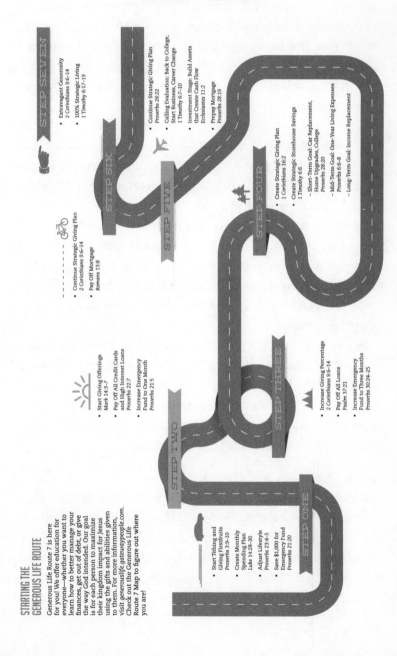

## STARTING THE GENEROUS LIFE ROUTE

Generous Life Route 7 is here for you! We offer education for everyone—whether you want to learn how to better manage your finances, get out of debt, or give the way God intended. Our goal is for each person to maximize their kingdom impact for Jesus using the gifts and abilities given to them. For more information, visit generouslife.gatewaypeople.com. Check out the Generous Life Route 7 Map to figure out where you are!

**STEP ONE**
- Start Tithing and Giving Firstfruits
  *Proverbs 3:9–10*
- Create Monthly Spending Plan
  *Luke 14:28–30*
- Adjust Lifestyle
  *Proverbs 23:4–5*
- Save $1,000 for Emergency Fund
  *Proverbs 21:20*

**STEP TWO**
- Start Giving Offerings
  *Mark 14:3–7*
- Pay Off All Credit Cards and High Interest Loans
  *Proverbs 22:7*
- Increase Emergency Fund to One Month
  *Proverbs 21:5*

**STEP THREE**
- Increase Giving Percentage
  *2 Corinthians 9:6–14*
- Pay Off All Loans
  *Psalm 37:21*
- Increase Emergency Fund to Three Months
  *Proverbs 30:24–25*

**STEP FOUR**
- Create Strategic Giving Plan
  *1 Corinthians 16:2*
- Create Strategic Storehouse Savings
  *1 Timothy 6:6*
  - Short-Term Goal: Car Replacement, Home Upgrades, College
    *Proverbs 28:20*
  - Mid-Term Goal: One-Year Living Expenses
    *Proverbs 6:6–8*
  - Long-Term Goal: Income Replacement

**STEP FIVE**
- Continue Strategic Giving Plan
  *2 Corinthians 9:6–14*
- Pay Off Mortgage
  *Romans 13:8*

**STEP SIX**
- Continue Strategic Giving Plan
  *Proverbs 28:22*
- Calling Evaluation: Back to College, Start Business, Career Change
  *1 Timothy 6:7–10*
- Investment Stage: Build Assets that Create Cash Flow
  *Ecclesiastes 11:2*
- Prepay Mortgage
  *Proverbs 28:19*

**STEP SEVEN**
- Extravagant Generosity
  *2 Corinthians 9:6–14*
- 100% Strategic Living
  *1 Timothy 6:17–19*

Beginning in this chapter, we will be using what I've called the Route 7 Road Map. This is a tool to help you apply biblical principles to your finances in a simple and systematic way. When you set out on a long drive across the country a GPS system is a useful tool because it gives you turn-by-turn directions. Consider the Route 7 Road Map your GPS for navigating the generous life journey.

As you can see from the illustration, the map has seven steps with substeps to complete on the journey. Within each step are giving, spending, and saving elements specific to that leg of the journey. You will also find verses to help anchor the financial principles to the Bible.

Everyone starts the generous life journey in a different location, so study the road map to assess where you are and which steps you still need to complete. We have seen this map work for families in all stages of life and financial positions, and I'm confident it will work for you too, if you follow along without skipping any steps.

Before I set off on a trip I personally like to see the entire route. Then, knowing the overall path, I feel more comfortable following turn-by-turn instruction. That's why I am outlining the entire road map here within step one, even though we will address each step as we move along through the book. So let's take a brief look at each leg of our journey.

### Step 1: The basics

Every journey starts somewhere and these initial goals within step 1 open the door to God's blessing in your financial future. Step 1 is a fundamental building block, so I recommend that you complete all the goals of this step. Do not move to step 2 if you have not implemented each of the four goals in step 1.

*Start tithing, or giving firstfruits offerings.*

> Honor the LORD with your possessions, and with the firstfruits of all your increase; so your barns will be filled with plenty and your vats will overflow with new wine.
>
> —PROVERBS 3:9–10

*Create a monthly spending plan.*

> Suppose one of you wants to build a tower. Won't you first sit down and estimate the cost to see if you have enough money to complete it? For if you lay the foundation and are not able to finish it, everyone who sees it will ridicule you, saying, "This person began to build and wasn't able to finish."
>
> —LUKE 14:28–30, NIV

*Adjust your lifestyle to live beneath, or at least within, your means.*

> Do not wear yourself out to get rich; do not trust your own cleverness. Cast but a glance at riches, and they are gone, for they will surely sprout wings and fly off to the sky like an eagle.
>
> —PROVERBS 23:4–5

*Save $1,000 toward an emergency fund.*

> There is precious treasure and oil in the dwelling of the wise, but a foolish man swallows it up.
>
> —PROVERBS 21:20, NAS

**Step 2: Begin breaking the bondage to debt.**

Step two has a high intensity focus on getting out of debt while dedicating a percentage of available funds to increasing savings. I recommend paying off debt and saving at the same time to use your growing savings to keep you out of debt in the future. Many families experience a debt cycle because they never have the savings to cover emergencies that occur while trying to get out of debt. Use a debt snowball approach listing your debts smallest to largest in size, paying the smallest first then moving that payment to the next. If the debts are the same size go for the higher interest rate first. Set aside a percentage to give over your tithe and watch the miracle of multiplication begin to happen in your finances. Automatically direct an amount into your savings account until you reach one month living expense then move that saving draft amount back to debt repayment until it is gone. Incrementally you will see the financial bondage getting lighter and lighter.

*Start giving offerings over and above the tithe.*

See Mark 14:3–7 for an example of extravagant giving.

*Pay off all credit cards and high-interest loans.*

> The rich rule over the poor, and the borrower is slave to the lender.
> —PROVERBS 22:7, NIV

*Increase savings to one-month of living expenses.*

**Step 3: Grow in freedom.**
Now that the high interest credit card debt is paid off, your savings is up to one month of living expenses, and your giving is growing as a percentage, it is time to eliminate other all other debts excluding the mortgage. Consider increasing giving by a percentage that fits in your budget. Then build your savings to a full three months of expenses. By the end of this stage you should feel very good about your direction. You'll have no debt other than the mortgage, your

savings will be growing, and that feeling of freedom should be growing too.

*Increase giving percentage.*

> A generous person will prosper; whoever refreshes others will be refreshed.
>
> —PROVERBS 11:25

*Pay off all loans.*

> The wicked borrow and do not repay, but the righteous give generously.
>
> —PSALM 37:21

*Increase emergency fund to three months of living expenses.*

> Four things on earth are small, yet they are extremely wise: Ants are creatures of little strength, yet they store up their food in the summer.
>
> —PROVERBS 30:24–25

**Step 4: Focus on saving.**

Now that the debts are paid off it is time to get very strategic about saving and giving money. Savings should be focused toward short-, medium-, and long-term goals. In the same way your giving should be very strategic. Your giving goals should be clarified according to your God-given passions. Do you have a heart for a certain region of missions? Is there a specific ministry you would like to support? The goal in this step is to be laser focused on intentional giving and saving.

*Create a strategic giving plan.*

> On the first day of every week, each one of you should set aside a sum of money in keeping with your income, saving it up, so that when I come no collections will have to be made.
>
> —1 CORINTHIANS 16:2

*Build a strategic fund for savings storehouse.*

> But godliness with contentment is great gain.
>
> —1 TIMOTHY 6:6

- Short-term savings goal: car replacement, home upgrades, college fund

> A faithful person will be richly blessed, but one eager to get rich will not go unpunished.
>
> —PROVERBS 28:20, NIV

- Mid-term savings goal: one-year living expenses

> Go to the ant, you sluggard; consider its ways and be wise! It has no commander, no overseer or ruler, yet it stores its provisions in summer and gathers its food at harvest.
>
> —PROVERBS 6:6–8, NIV

Long-term savings goal: replace income through cash-flowing investments

> In the morning sow your seed, and in the evening do not withhold your hand; for you do not know which will prosper, either this or that, or whether both alike will be good.
>
> —ECCLESIASTES 11:6

**Step 5: Begin to prepay mortgage and invest.**

As your savings grows and your freedom increases, this is a great time to reevaluate your calling as you build upon the solid foundation that has been laid. If you are in the right career calling for this season then began to pay off the mortgage if you have one. Why wait until this stage to begin prepaying off the mortgage? If there were an income emergency, like a layoff, and you had no savings, you risk losing the home to the lender, including all your hard-earned equity. This is also a great time in your financial journey to create investments that provide cash flow. Design a financial plan to use your assets to build additional assets. When you're ready to invest, I recommend contacting a Qualified Kingdom Advisor through author Ron Blue's ministry to discuss options that fit your specific financial situation (www .kingdomadvisors.org).

*Continue your strategic giving plan.*

The stingy are eager to get rich and are unaware that poverty awaits them.

—Proverbs 28:22, NIV

*Evaluate your calling. (Is the Lord calling you to go back to college, start a business, or change careers?)*

For we brought nothing into the world, and we can take nothing out of it. But if we have food and clothing, we will be content with that. Those who want to get rich fall into temptation and a trap and into many foolish and harmful desires that plunge people into ruin and destruction. For the love of money is a root of all kinds of evil. Some people, eager for money, have wandered from the faith and pierced themselves with many griefs.

—1 TIMOTHY 6:7–10, NIV

*Invest (build assets that create cash flow).*

Invest in seven ventures, yes, in eight; you do not know what disaster may come upon the land.

—ECCLESIASTES 11:2, NIV

*Begin paying extra toward your mortgage.*

Those who work their land will have abundant food, but those who chase fantasies will have their fill of poverty.

—PROVERBS 28:19, NIV

**Step 6: Live debt-free.**

In this stage finish paying off that mortgage and celebrate a milestone that few people ever experience. With that, you'll be on a roll! Continue to fine tune your savings and giving plans.

*Continue your strategic giving plan.*

Remember this: Whoever sows sparingly will also reap sparingly, and whoever sows generously will also reap generously. Each of you should give what you have decided in your heart to give, not reluctantly or under compulsion, for God loves a cheerful giver. And God is able to bless you abundantly, so that in all things at all times, having all that you need, you will abound in every good work. As it is written: "They have freely scattered their gifts to the poor; their righteousness endures forever."

Now he who supplies seed to the sower and bread for food will also supply and increase your store of seed and will enlarge the harvest of your righteousness. You will be enriched in every way so that you can be generous on every occasion, and through us your generosity will result in thanksgiving to God. This service that you perform is not only supplying the needs of the Lord's people but is also overflowing in many expressions of thanks to God. Because of the service by which you have proved yourselves, others will praise God for the obedience that accompanies your confession of the gospel of Christ, and for your generosity in sharing with them and with everyone else. And in their prayers for you their hearts will go out to you, because of the surpassing grace God has given you.

—2 Corinthians 9:6–14, niv

*Pay off mortgage.*

Let no debt remain outstanding, except the continuing debt to love one another, for whoever loves others has fulfilled the law.

—Romans 13:8, niv

## Step 7: Live strategically and give extravagantly.

Can you imagine how it will feel to be free of all debt, including the mortgage, and have a fully funded emergency fund with savings for future major purchases, investment accounts that are working for you, and giving tailored to your God-given passions? This would be a fantastic place from which to live out the kingdom call on your life. Think for a minute of all you could do in this position. I venture to say you would be fully living the generous life!

*Practice extravagant generosity.*

I have shown you in every way, by laboring like this, that you must support the weak. And remember the words of the Lord Jesus, that He said, "It is more blessed to give than to receive."

—ACTS 20:35

*Live 100 percent strategically.*

Command those who are rich in this present age not to be haughty, nor to trust in uncertain riches but in the living God, who gives us richly all things to enjoy. Let them do good, that they be rich in good works, ready to give, willing to share, storing up for themselves a good foundation for the time to come, that they may lay hold on eternal life.

—1 TIMOTHY 6:17–19

### Route 7 Road Map Step 1

- Start tithing, or giving firstfruits offerings.

- Create a monthly spending plan.

- Adjust your lifestyle to live beneath, or at least within, your means.

- Save $1,000 toward an emergency fund.

## YOUR ROUTE 7 ACTION PLAN

Step 7 of the Route 7 Road Map is an awesome place to be financially. But in order to get there, you must be intentional. It won't happen by accident. As we prepare to set off on the generous life journey, I want you to think about your goals by answering the following questions.

- What is God calling you to do?

- Where would you like to be financially, and how quickly would you like to get there?

- What obstacles are keeping you from meeting those goals?

It's OK if you're not sure of the answers. Just thinking about them is a great place to start. By the end of our journey together, I believe you will have clear answers for each of those questions. But right now I want to commit to begin tithing if you're not already doing so. I guarantee that if you commit to giving God the firstfruits of your income, your life and finances will never be the same. Don't believe me? Keep reading.

# Chapter 4

# FIRST THINGS FIRST

G IVING. I CAN picture you wincing and groaning just seeing that simple word. Most people do when they hear anything about tithing, giving, or being generous because they've been wounded in this area. As I said earlier, there's been a lot of wrong teaching about giving.

God's heart is not to make you feel guilty or put you under condemnation about giving. I promise never to point my finger and yell at you about the amount you put in the offering plate. Romans 8:1 tells us "there is therefore now no condemnation to those who are in Christ Jesus."

Using guilt and condemnation to get people to give is simply not fair. It robs them of the joy of the whole experience. So let's get rid of all condemnation in the area of giving, whether it's from people in the church or from within ourselves. Condemnation is the hammer of the enemy. It's the tool he uses to beat us down and take us further from God.

In my teaching and counseling, I've observed that most people are like a piñata when it comes to giving. They're not balanced—they swing from one side to the other. They're either completely for it or completely against it.

This is all part of the enemy's game. If he can stop people from tithing and giving, by whatever means, they'll miss out on many of the blessings God wants to bring into their lives—and then the devil will try to get them to blame God for their adverse circumstances.

On the flipside, if people do become generous in their giving, the enemy will make them feel guilty about the resources they choose to keep. People with a generous heart give to serve the Lord but then worry they're not doing enough. Everyone who is generous struggles with this.

## THE ROOT OF GENEROSITY

Biblical generosity is rooted in love. God set the example throughout the Bible, and it culminates in John 3:16.

> For God so loved the world that He gave His only begotten Son, that whoever believes in Him should not perish, but have eternal life.
>
> —MEV

In Romans 5:8 we learn, "God demonstrates his own love for us in this: while we were still sinners, Christ died for us." Because of His love, God gave His Son, Jesus. And it was because of Jesus's love for us that He willingly died for our sins. Love is what motivated God to give, and the early church followed this example. Paul wrote:

> And now, brothers, we want you to know about the grace that God has given the Macedonian churches. Out of the most severe trial, their overflowing joy and their extreme poverty welled up in rich generosity. For I testify that they gave as much as they were able, and even beyond their ability. Entirely on their own, they urgently pleaded with us for the privilege of sharing in this service to the saints.
>
> —2 CORINTHIANS 8:1–4

In the midst of severe trial and extreme poverty, they still had overwhelming joy in Christ—and they gave.

At its core, generosity is a heart issue. Before they entered the Promised Land, Moses gave the Israelites a lesson on the link between the condition of their hearts and God's blessing.

> However, there should be no poor among you, for in the land the Lord your God is giving you to possess as your inheritance, he will richly bless you, *if* only you fully obey the Lord your God and are careful to follow all these commands I am giving you today. For the Lord your God will bless you as he promised, and you will lend to many nations but will borrow from none. You will rule over many nations but none will rule over you.
> —Deuteronomy 15:4–6, niv, emphasis added

God directly connected His blessing to the condition of the Israelites' hearts—whether they were willing to obey Him fully. Deuteronomy 15 goes on to identify four types of hearts. Everyone who goes on a generosity journey falls into one of these four categories at some point in time.

## 1. The selfish heart

> If anyone is poor among your fellow Israelites in any of the towns of the land the Lord your God is giving you, do not be *hardhearted or tightfisted* toward them. Rather, be openhanded and freely lend them whatever they need. Be careful not to harbor this wicked thought: "The seventh year, the year for canceling debts, is near," so that you do not show ill will toward the needy among your fellow Israelites and give them nothing. They may then appeal to the Lord against you, and you will be found guilty of sin.
> —Deuteronomy 15:7–9, emphasis added

The selfish or tightfisted heart was me early in my walk with the Lord when I first heard teachings on giving. I thought I was generous, but I wasn't. I was focused on myself and any giving I did was done reluctantly. I wasn't concerned with where the gift was going or what it accomplished. It was all about me.

## 2. The grudging heart

> Give generously to him and do so without a *grudging heart*; then because of this the LORD your God will bless you in all your work and in everything you put your hand to. There will always be poor in the land. Therefore I command you to be openhanded toward your brothers and toward the poor and needy in your land.
>
> DEUTERONOMY 15:10–11, NIV, EMPHASIS ADDED

The grudging or grieving heart says, "I'll try giving, but I'll be grieved about it." There is a level of resentment about giving. We give out of coerced obedience, not out of a heart that loves and wants to serve. In this category, we forget that when we cheerfully obey His Word, God can do something great.

## 3. The generous heart

> If a fellow Hebrew, a man or a woman, sells himself to you and serves you six years, in the seventh year you must let him go free. And when you release him, do not send him away empty-handed. Supply him *generously* from your flock, your threshing floor and your wine-press. Give to him as the LORD your God has blessed you.
>
> DEUTERONOMY 15:12–14, NIV, EMPHASIS ADDED

The generous heart enjoys giving. Matthew 6:21 reminds us, "For where your treasure is, there will your heart be also" (MEV).

## 4. The grateful heart

> You shall remember that you were a slave in the land of
> Egypt, and *the LORD your God redeemed you*; therefore
> I command you this thing today.
> —DEUTERONOMY 15:15, EMPHASIS ADDED

The grateful heart sees giving as the way to express our thankfulness to God for all He has done for us and given us. All around me, I see the wrecked lives and messes created by people who haven't walked with Jesus, who haven't stepped into this blessed life. And while I grieve for them and help them however I can, it makes me glad I'm a giver. When I think about what a mess my life was before Christ and how far the Lord has brought me, I settle into a grateful frame of mind.

The Scriptures say there will always be poor in the land (Mark 14:7, John 12:8). Why? Is it only because people make poor decisions and don't handle money wisely?

In my former church I counseled a middle-aged man who was somewhat mentally challenged. He was able to work and pretty much take care of himself, but he couldn't handle his finances. He was constantly in a financial crisis or on the brink of one. I negotiated with utility and credit card companies on his behalf, which kept him going until the next crisis hit. But our plans always imploded.

Once he received a lump sum settlement of $80,000, yet was soon back to see me with another financial crisis. When I asked him what happened to the settlement, he told me he spent it on baseball cards.

I vented to the lead pastor about this—we pastors do this from time to time, you know—questioning why this man was in my life.

My pastor said, "You don't know?"

"No," I said. "And I wouldn't mind if he was out of my life."

But my pastor said, "He's in your life for you."

This stopped me short because I thought the pastor had gone crazy. Then he explained that the poor are in the land to test our hearts. What are we going to do? How are we going to help them? And this is the question that really nailed me— what will our *attitudes* be as we do it?

Will our hearts be grateful, generous, grieving, or selfish?

When people are habitually in crisis, the problem is not financial. It's spiritual. The enemy is using a poverty mentality or some other weapon to keep that person in bondage.

It's the church's responsibility to take care of the poor, not the government's. God wants the church not only to help meet people's immediate needs but also to mentor the poor so they can be delivered from the bondage of poverty and walk fully in all God has for them.

God's heart is for the poor. Our job is to join Him in ministering to them. If your brother is in need and you don't help him, Deuteronomy 15:9 says he could appeal to the Lord against you, and you could be found guilty of sin. That doesn't sound like fun to me.

## DEVELOPING A GENEROUS AND GRATEFUL HEART

How do we develop a generous and grateful heart? We do it by applying the Principle of the First to our income. This is not only a powerful standard to live by, it is also a test—one we face every time we get paid.

Proverbs 3:5–6 tells us, "Trust in the LORD with all your heart and lean not on your own understanding; in all your ways acknowledge Him, and He will make direct your paths" (MEV).

Throughout all the Scriptures, God gives us vivid object lessons of His ownership and our stewardship responsibilities, and foretold of a coming Messiah. The whole Bible is an object lesson about Jesus. If you find something in the Scripture you don't understand, just think, "It's about Jesus," and that will help you figure it out.

Even the Principle of the First is about Jesus. Follow along with me as we look at this principle in God's Word.

> Then the LORD spoke to Moses, saying: Sanctify unto Me all the firstborn, the firstborn of every womb among the children of Israel, both of man and of beast. It is Mine."
> —EXODUS 13:1–2, MEV

> That you shall set apart to the LORD the first offspring of every womb and the first offspring of every beast which you have. The males shall be the LORD's. But every first offspring of a donkey you shall redeem with a lamb. And if you do not redeem it, then you shall break its neck, and all the firstborn of man among your sons you shall redeem.
> —EXODUS 13:12–13, MEV

Every time one of their animals delivered its firstborn, the Israelites had to sacrifice it, or if it was unclean they had to redeem it with a lamb. To give you some perspective, in the ancient Hebrew culture the donkey was considered unclean while the lamb was treasured.

The practice of sacrificing the firstborn is not common in our culture, so we tend not to see the significance of this. But the Principle of the First is seen throughout Scripture.

God's portion was devoted, or consecrated, to Him at the Temple. And He commanded the firstborn be sacrificed or redeemed. This set the stage for the most important firstborn sacrifice. Jesus was the Lamb of God and His firstborn Son. He was clean and we were unclean, so He was sacrificed so we could be redeemed.

After Jesus's death and resurrection, the New Testament

church met on Sunday because of the Principle of the First. They gave the first day of the week to the Lord.

The premise of the Principle of the First is that firstfruits must be offered to God.

> The first of the *firstfruits* of your land you shall bring into the house of the LORD your God.
>
> —EXODUS 23:19, EMPHASIS ADDED

> Honor the LORD with your possessions, and with the *firstfruits* of all your increase; so your barns will be filled with plenty, and your vats will overflow with new wine.
>
> —PROVERBS 3:9–10, EMPHASIS ADDED

Because God's portion is given to the temple, it is blessed. If the firstfruits are not given to God, they are cursed because they are stolen.

Let's see how the Principle of the First applied in the example of Cain and Abel.

> In the course of time Cain brought an offering to the LORD of the fruit of the ground. Abel also brought the firstborn of his flock and of their fat portions. And the LORD had respect for Abel and for his offering, but for Cain and for his offering, He did not have respect. And Cain was very angry and his countenance fell.
>
> —GENESIS 4:3–5, MEV

Why did God accept Abel's offering and not Cain's? Cain's was not his firstfruits. He violated the Principle of the First. The Bible says *in the process of time* Cain brought the fruit of the ground. That was not the firstfruit. It was just what he felt like bringing at the time.

Abel, on the other hand, did follow the Principle of the First.

He brought the firstborn of his flock. And God honored him because he honored God.

## THE TITHE MUST BE BROUGHT FIRST

I can hear the *Dragnet* theme rolling around in your mind. But bear with me, and I think you'll see how important this ordinance is to God and how it can affect not only your finances but also your relationship with Him.

An ordinance simply means a decree of ordinary behavior. God wants tithing to be as natural to us as breathing.

The tithe is 10 percent of our income. It is a fixed amount. The firstfruits is a position—it comes first. So this means we bring the first ten percent of our income to God.

In the Old Testament, during the time of King Hezekiah's reign, the temple had fallen into disarray and society had run amok. While cleaning out the temple, the Israelites discovered the scrolls of the law and brought them to Hezekiah. He ordered that they be read to the people, and revival broke out as the Hebrews heard the law and applied it to every area of their lives.

> And when the command spread, the sons of Israel *gave generously* the *first fruits* of grain, wine, oil, honey, and all the produce of the field. And they *brought* in abundance a *tenth portion* of everything.
> —2 CHRONICLES 31:5, MEV, EMPHASIS ADDED

As the Israelites began to honor the Lord with their firsts, everything flourished around them. The church needs to rediscover the Principle of the First, which begins with the tithe. As they do, the Lord will begin to bless them. Then they can start to rediscover the principles of stewardship and watch what God does in the society around them through their faithful generosity. I guarantee it will be transformational.

This is already evident in my church. Gateway Church is an extremely generous church full of people who are giving radically. Many surveys show that Gateway's members give at a level that is double and even triple that of most churches. This is because the people have been taught the truth about tithing and are choosing to follow God's way. I'm looking forward to seeing how we impact society over the next twenty years as we plant churches and raise up congregations that follow these same principles of giving.

God instituted the Principle of the First because He knew it would serve as both a filtering and strengthening process for our hearts. And He knew it would bless and create spiritual revival in a community. He says in His Word:

> From the days of your fathers you have gone away from My ordinances and have not kept them. Return to Me, and I will return to you, says the LORD of Hosts. But you say, "How shall we return?" Will a man rob God? Yet you have robbed Me. But you say, "How have we robbed You?" In tithes and offerings. You are cursed with a curse, your whole nation, for you are robbing Me. Bring all the tithes into the storehouse, that there may be food in My house, and test Me now in this, says the LORD of Hosts, if I will not open for you the windows of heaven and pour out for you a blessing, that there will not be room enough to receive it. I will rebuke the devourer for your sakes, so that it will not destroy the fruit of your ground, and the vines in your field will not fail to bear fruit, says the LORD of Hosts. Then all the nations will call you blessed, for you will be a delightful land, says the LORD of Hosts.
>
> —MALACHI 3:7–12, MEV

God was telling them they had turned away from His ordinances, His system of ordinary behavior. But if they returned, they would be blessed. He even challenged them to test Him. He was saying, "Do it and see what happens."

While we're talking about Malachi 3:7, which is a well-known passage used to instruct concerning tithing and giving, let me make a quick note. The tithe is never "given"; it is always *brought* or *returned*. God gives us an income, or a harvest, and we return the first 10 percent to Him.

You may be wondering, "How can I give something that is not mine?" Think about it this way. Suppose I loaned my car to a friend. What would he do when he was finished using it? He can't "give" me the car, because it's already mine. He can only return it to me.

In the same way, the tithe is not mine. All the increase we are given is from God—it's His, just like the car in my previous example. We don't "give" Him 10 percent of the income He provides. We "return" the tithe. And it's clear in Deuteronomy 12:5–17 and 14:22–29 that the tithe goes to the house of God. Why? Malachi 3:10 says to bring all the tithes into the storehouse, which is God's house, "that there may be food in My house."

Some people think of this "food" as God's Word, but this verse is referring to more than spiritual sustenance. Acts 4:34–35 describes how there were no needy people among the early church because the congregation would bring money to the apostles to give to those in need. God blesses us so we can be His arms and feet extended and bless others.

We will discuss the power of the generous life as we move through this book. But right now I want to address some common questions about the tithe.

## COMMON QUESTIONS ABOUT TITHING

**Isn't tithing part of the Old Testament law?**

The principle of the tithe supersedes the law. Abel, the first tither, gave a tithe 2,500 years before the law.

For another example, look at what transpired between Abraham and Melchizedek:

> Then Melchizedek king of Salem brought out bread and wine. He was the priest of God Most High. And he blessed him and said, "Blessed be Abram by God Most High, Creator of heaven and earth; and blessed be God Most High, who has delivered your enemies into your hand." Then Abram gave him a tenth of everything.
> —GENESIS 14:18–20, MEV

Abraham, our spiritual father, tithed to Melchizedek. This took place long before God gave the law to Moses. And Jacob tithed four hundred years before the law:

> Then this stone, which I have set for a pillar, will be the house of God, and from all that You give me I will surely give a tenth to You.
> —GENESIS 28:22, MEV

Is murder part of the law? Yes. The Ten Commandments clearly say, "Thou shalt not kill." Was murder OK prior to the law? No. Cain was punished for killing Abel. So now that we no longer live under the law but under grace, can we kill each other? No. It's still not right.

The function of the law is to bring us to Christ. Galatians 3:24 tells us, "Therefore the law was our tutor to bring us to Christ, that we might be justified by faith."

If I hadn't been challenged to tithe, I would not have grown in my relationship with Jesus. I don't think I'd be a pastor today. In fact, I'm sure I'd be a self-centered businessman, and I would not have grown spiritually or experienced the joys of taking the generous life journey. The law did exactly what it was supposed to do in my life. It convicted me and drew me closer to Jesus.

Romans 15:4 says, "For whatever things were written before were written for our learning, that we through the patience and comfort of the Scriptures might have hope." All things in the Word are written for our learning, growing, and understanding. We can actually rip out that divider between the Old and New Testaments. All sixty-six books share the same central message—they all point us to Jesus as the way to live a blessed life here on earth and experience the eternal life to follow.

Second Timothy 3:16–17 tells us that "all Scripture is given by inspiration of God, and is profitable for doctrine, for reproof, for correction, for instruction in righteousness, that the man of God may be complete, thoroughly equipped for every good work." In the denomination I grew up in, we discounted the Old Testament when making theological decisions. We were taught the Old Testament, but we focused on Matthew through Revelation for guidance in our daily lives. We included Psalms and Proverbs because they were nice.

This actually did me a great disservice because it caused me not to fully understand the Spirit of the Lord. I thought God had changed His mind in the New Testament and had given us a new set of rules. But God's Word hasn't changed. It's exciting when we discover how integrated the Scriptures really are. The New Testament is concealed in the Old Testament, and the Old Testament is revealed in the New Testament.

Just in case you're from a church similar to the one I grew up in, let me be clear: tithing is in the New Testament. Jesus and Paul both affirm the tithe. Matthew's Gospel is in the New Testament, and in it Jesus spoke the following words.

> Woe to you, scribes and Pharisees, hypocrites [and other
> miscellaneous jerks]! You tithe mint and dill and cumin,
> but have neglected the weightier matters of the law: jus-
> tice and mercy and faith. These you ought to have done
> without leaving the others undone.
> —MATTHEW 23:23, MEV; SEE ALSO LUKE 12:34

Jesus taught that tithing is still part of what we're called to
do. And as if that weren't enough, in Hebrews 7:1–8, we learn
that Melchizedek is an Old Testament type of Jesus.

> For this Melchizedek, king of Salem, priest of the Most
> High God, met Abraham returning from the slaughter
> of the kings and blessed him. To him Abraham also gave
> a tenth part of everything. In the first place, his name is
> translated "king of righteousness," and then also he is
> king of Salem, which means "king of peace." Without
> father, without mother, without descent, having neither
> beginning of days nor end of life, but made like the Son
> of God, he continually remains a priest.
>
> Now consider how great this man was, to whom even
> the patriarch Abraham gave a tenth of the spoils. Surely
> the sons of Levi, who receive the office of the priesthood,
> have a command to take tithes of the people according
> to the law, that is, from their brothers, though they also
> come from the seed of Abraham. But this man, whose
> descent is not numbered among them, received tithes
> from Abraham and blessed him who had the promises.
> Without question, the inferior is blessed by the superior.
> In the one case mortal men receive tithes, but in the other
> he of whom it is witnessed that he is alive receives them.
> —HEBREWS 7:1–8, MEV

Today mortal men receive and administer the tithe. This is
a big deal that every pastor must take seriously. We are a spiritual priesthood of the lineage of the Levites, administering

the gifts of the people to further God's kingdom. This is a heavy responsibility for the pastoral ministry, one that should be taken seriously.

**When do you pay the tithe?**

Believe it or not, it is possible to give 10 percent of your "increase" (which is generally your income) and not be tithing. Here's how. Let's say you get paid on Thursday. You pay all your bills and then buy groceries. Then you write the tithe check before you go to church on Sunday. In this scenario the firstfruits were given to pay bills and buy groceries.

It is my firm belief that the tithe should be the first check we write, or the first payment we make, after we receive our income. Let's be honest, are we really giving in faith when we give 10 percent *after* we've paid all our bills? Aren't we revealing *our* priorities when we *willingly* pay everybody else and then see if there's enough left over to bring God His portion?

There are so many blessings that go along with tithing, but they only work when we *put God first*. It's the principle of faith that initiates the blessings.

**Do we tithe on the gross or the net?**

I believe and teach we should tithe on our gross income. If I'm wrong, I'd rather be on the side of generosity. Besides, who do you think will bless your money: the government or God?

**Does the entire tithe go to the church?**

Malachi 3:10 tells us to "bring all the tithes to the storehouse." The storehouse is God's house. How do we know?

> Then there will be *a place which the LORD your God will choose to cause His name to dwell*. There you must bring all that I command you: your burnt offerings, and your

> sacrifices, your *tithes,* the offering of your hand, and all
> your choice vows which you vow to the LORD.
> —DEUTERONOMY 12:11, MEV, EMPHASIS ADDED

God's house is a place of provision both spiritually and naturally. As I mentioned previously, we read in Acts 4:34–35 that there were no needy people among the early church because the congregation brought money to the apostles to give to those in need. It's clear the tithe goes to the church—the place God calls home and the instrument He uses to bless others.

### Should I get out of debt before I begin tithing?

If you're determined to get out of debt, you'll want God on your side. You'll want His blessing on your finances so you can get out of debt more quickly. The way to experience God's blessing on your finances is to trust in Him with all your heart and honor Him with your firstfruits, as Proverbs 3:5–6, 9–10 instructs.

### Should I tithe if my spouse doesn't want to do so?

At one seminar I taught, a couple sat on the front row, and I could tell the husband did not want to be there. Based on his posture he thought my teaching was a huge waste of his time. He sat with his arms crossed, not taking notes, looking like he'd rather have a root canal without anesthesia!

His wife, on the other hand, was leaning forward, writing down everything I said and giving her husband the occasional elbow when I made a point she really liked. When I reached the Q&A part of the session, she lifted her hand and asked the first question: "I want to tithe but my husband won't let me. Are my finances cursed? He doesn't want to give to the church. I want to know—do I follow God or do I follow my husband?"

His eyes were as big as saucers. Everyone held their breath. You could have heard a pin drop. I think he was too shocked to say anything. I'll tell you, I really wanted to be a fly on the window during that drive home!

The Lord gave me the grace and wisdom to answer her. I explained that God had put a structure in a marriage: the husband is the head of the household. If she and her husband were not in agreement on something, I told her it was her responsibility to honor her husband's wishes. On the flipside, because the husband is the head of the household, if he wanted to tithe and his wife didn't, I believe he would be within biblical grounds to tithe despite his wife's objections.

However, sometimes as spouses we have to duck and pray. We have to get out of the way so God can have a clear shot at our husband or wife. My advice is, if you're not in unity, and an issue is adding stress to your relationship, take a break. Step aside and pray about the situation and see where God leads. These principles are not in place to drive a wedge between people. They were instituted to draw people closer to each other and to God.

### What if I just don't want to tithe?

Then don't. But your issue is deeper than tithing. Tithing and giving are indicators of the condition of our hearts, and when we put God first, we are blessed. It's as simple as that.

I'm not trying to talk you into tithing. I'm explaining the principles God has given us throughout His Word for living a life fully blessed. I can't force you into it. God wants us to give willingly and cheerfully. So if you don't want to tithe, don't tithe. It's your choice. But I would rather live on 90 percent that is all redeemed and blessed than on 100 percent that is all cursed. Wouldn't you?

## A Cycle of Giving

In some circles ministers teach that we should give to receive God's abundant blessings. Give extravagantly and you will reap extravagantly, they say. And there is truth in that statement. But too often we focus so much on receiving financial increase that we miss the real reason God blesses us.

We're blessed so we can create reciprocal relationships. God blesses us, and we in turn bless others. It becomes a cycle through which everyone benefits.

The problem arises when we become a reservoir instead of a conduit.

God blesses, and we raise our lifestyle.

God blesses, and we buy extravagant jewelry.

God blesses, and the next thing you know, we're driving a Rolls Royce.

There is nothing wrong with having nice things, but obtaining more material possessions should not be the reason for our giving. God is not a genie who can be manipulated with tithes and offerings into making us abundantly rich. Giving to get isn't God's plan. Giving to get is materialism dressed up in church clothes.

Look at what the Apostle Paul had to say about giving.

> Remember this: Whoever sows sparingly will also reap sparingly, and whoever sows generously will also reap generously. Each man should give what he has decided in his heart to give, not reluctantly or under compulsion, for God loves a cheerful giver. And God is able to make *all* grace abound to you, so that in *all* things at *all* times, having *all* that you need, *you will abound in every good work.* As it is written: "He has scattered abroad his gifts to the poor; his righteousness endures forever." Now he who supplies seed to the sower and bread for

food will also supply and increase your store of seed and will enlarge the harvest of your righteousness. You will be made rich in every way so that *you can be generous on every occasion,* and through us your generosity will result in thanksgiving to God.

—2 CORINTHIANS 9:6–11, NIV, EMPHASIS ADDED

Did you notice how many times the word "all" was used? This is an amazing passage, one that I'd encourage you to stick it on the dashboard of your car or on your refrigerator so you can remind yourself of the reason God calls us to give. It's not so we can amass wealth so we can feel secure for the future. It's not so we can impress others with our stuff. And it's certainly not so we can feel valuable or successful. By being cheerful givers, Paul tells us we are made rich in every way (not just financially) *so we can be generous.*

I want to draw your attention to one other key in this passage. These verses point to two types of giving over and above the tithe: *offerings* and *extravagant offerings.* Offerings are what we give over our 10 percent tithe. Extravagant offerings are large gifts that are sometimes hard to rationalize and possibly even scary but are nonetheless very satisfying and rewarding. Even if it seems crazy, when you know you've heard from God about giving a certain amount, obeying Him is always the right thing to do! Abraham's willingness to offer Isaac was an extravagant offering. God sending Jesus to die for our sins—that was an extravagant offering! God will expand your seed when you are looking to expand His kingdom.

Remember Luke 19 and the parable of the talents? Which steward received the other steward's talent? It was the one who already had ten talents—the one who did the best with what he had been given and multiplied the Master's resources. If we don't get giving right, it will become a hindrance in all areas of our finances, all areas of our relationships, and in all areas where God speaks into our lives.

I used to wonder if I was getting this whole generosity thing right in my own family. Was I setting the right example? Was I having a positive impact? And then God showed me something through my kids.

It was Christmastime, and my wife and I stopped at a Taco Bueno with the kids. There was an older woman working there, and we could see from her countenance and demeanor that something was not right. I asked her how she was doing.

She told us she was doing OK. She'd lost her husband a couple of years earlier and before then she'd never had to work outside the home. She was working now to earn some extra Christmas money, but she was struggling to save enough to bless her kids for Christmas. I offered to pray for her, but she declined and wandered on.

Our ten-year-old daughter said she wanted to give the woman all her money. She had saved $100 to buy a special bird. We agreed with her decision. As we headed home to get her money, the six-year-old and thirteen-year-old said they wanted to give too. Then I told my wife we needed to stop by the bank because I wanted to be part of this as well.

The kids really cleaned out everything for her. Along with the cash they included the "Bible bucks" they earned in children's ministry for bringing visitors or their Bibles to church as well as gift cards they'd received. My wife and I returned to the Taco Bueno and sent the kids in alone to give the woman the money. This was their idea, and we wanted them to experience the joy of giving their extravagant offering. They ran in and said to the woman, "Jesus wants to bless you." They gave her the envelope and ran off. They didn't know what else to do.

As we drove around the restaurant to leave, we glanced

in the window, and the woman was sobbing. And I thought, "Yeah, we're getting it right in this area for our kids."

This is the heart the Father wants to see in His people—not one that gives to get but one that seeks to use what God gives us to bless others.

---

### Route 7 Road Map Step 2

In this step, you will begin breaking the bondage to debt.

- Start giving offerings in addition to the tithe.
- Pay off all credit cards and high-interest loans.
- Increase savings to one-month of living expenses.

---

## YOUR ROUTE 7 ACTION PLAN

Now that you understand the importance God places on the tithe and how much He wants to use our obedience to bless us, I hope you'll be excited about giving God your firstfruits. As we move along in our generous life journey, I want you to continue to tithe and give as the Lord leads you. But at this point we are also going to start thinking about what God wants us to do with the remaining 90 percent. Chances are you won't be able to give generously if you have no financial margin, or surplus. That's why your Route 7 action step is to adjust your lifestyle to live within your means or, preferably, below your means.

If you've ever tried to live within a budget, you've probably faced the question, "How do I balance my budget if there isn't quite enough money to do everything I want?" There are really only three things you can do if more money goes out than comes in.

1. **Make more money**. This is what guys usually think of as the first response. Get a second job.

Work more hours. This is actually not the most efficient response because you tend to lose 30 to 35 percent of the extra money. You pay more in taxes, plus there's additional wear and tear on your cars and clothing, as well as other expenses. And think about how it affects your family and personal relationships.

2. **Spend less**. This is the most efficient way to balance your budget. Look carefully at where your money is going. You'll probably find some place to cut spending. You may be surprised by how much you spend on morning coffee, eating out, or vending snacks at work. But not everyone will find some place to cut costs. If you can't spend less or if lowering your spending doesn't seem to be doing the job quickly enough, consider putting some things up for sale.

3. **Sell stuff**. I admit, this can be difficult because some items have sentimental value. But for some, this is the best option to create more margin in their finances. Start by taking inventory of what you own. Is there anything you haven't used in a while? If so, sell it, especially if it's a high-ticket item. Set a time limit for yourself and determine that if the item hasn't been used it in "x" amount of time, you will sell it. But let me share a word of caution: This is also not always the most efficient way to balance your budget because it often is a one-time thing. You have just one desk collecting dust in the garage. You have just one junk car you can sell for parts. And there is always a chance you may need the

item again down the road—like that crib you were so sure you would never need again—and it could be more expensive to rebuy. One size doesn't fit all. I encourage everyone to seek the Lord for wisdom regarding their specific situation and follow His leading.

Ultimately your lifestyle decisions will determine the direction your life takes. There are basically four groups of people in the world.

## Group One

These are the ones who are living the life God called them to live with genuine satisfaction and are in good shape financially. If you're in this group, the pressure to make lifestyle adjustments is not as intense because you're on the mark. You're where you should be financially and steadily improving. In the Parable of the Sower (Matt. 13:1–9), this group is like the seed planted in fertile soil that receives thirty, sixty, and hundredfold returns.

## Group Two

These individuals are pursuing their calling in life but are in bad shape financially. The need to make some lifestyle changes is greater for this group because of the increased financial pressure they feel and the sense that they are setting a bad example in ministry, in their business or job, and in their family. In the Parable of the Sower, this group hears the Word, but their blessing is choked by the cares of this world.

## Group Three

These individuals are not pursuing their calling in life but are in good shape financially. The people in this group probably feel more spiritual pressure than financial pressure because they're not sure yet what God's called them to do, and they may be in some fear about what His calling may mean financially. In the Parable of the Sower, this group hears the Word but doesn't understand it, and as a result the word is snatched from their hearts.

When I was in construction, my wife and I intentionally lived beneath our means because I knew I was called to be a pastor, even though I wasn't in that season of life yet. I made a six-figure income, yet I drove one hundred-dollar cars—on purpose. I bought them for a hundred bucks, invested enough to get them started, and then drove them into the ground, which sometimes didn't take too long. I did this because I wanted to be in a position to move with God when He said, "Now is the time to step into full-time ministry." I didn't want to be concerned about how my wife and I would make it financially. That was the wisdom God gave me for that season, because when I entered the ministry I took a one hundred thousand-dollar pay cut. Yet my family was able to survive because my wife and I had made lifestyle decisions that put us in good shape both financially and spiritually.

This group needs to press in to God to see how He would

have them begin to walk in their calling. Or they need to prepare financially for the season when God will have them step out into their calling.

### Group Four

These are the ones who are not walking in their calling and are in bad shape financially. This group is following the recipe for pure frustration and disaster to a tee, and they are probably feeling intense pressure. Their lifestyle decisions are based on immediate and urgent needs—pay the rent, buy food, keep the electricity on. They are in survival mode and not experiencing the desires of their heart. In the Parable of the Sower, this group hears the Word, but it never takes root.

As you begin to budget and reorganize your finances, keep these four groups in mind. Pray that God will give you wisdom and the right strategy to move into Group One. Ask Him to show you how much to keep, how much to cut, and how radical you need to become to get on the right track financially.

Our lifestyle should bring us joy, not stress or frustration. If you're not enjoying your lifestyle, something needs to change.

The Bible does not define a Christian lifestyle; I wish it did. However, God did use all types of people to illustrate and establish His principles. He used the poor, the wealthy, the sick, the healthy, the maimed, the politicians, the soldiers, and the religious leaders to illustrate His truth. Our culture encourages us to spend all we make and more (which is why so many people have credit cards). It teaches us to be discontent because it attaches our self-worth to our net worth. These are all lies.

Paul sums up the truth beautifully in Philippians 4.

> I have learned to be content in whatever circumstances
> I am. I know how to get along with humble means, and
> I also know how to live in prosperity; in any and every

circumstance I have learned the secret of being filled and
going hungry, both of abundance and suffering need. I
can do all things through Him who strengthens me.
—PHILIPPIANS 4:11–13, NAS

Changing our lifestyles may seem like a daunting task,
but when we make Christ the central focus of our lives, He
strengthens us to do all He calls us to do.

If finding a way to pay your bills and have money left each
month still seems daunting to you, don't worry. In the next
chapter we will take a closer look at our spending and learn
how to get a handle on our finances. It involves making a clear
plan for how our money is spent—meaning we give every
dollar a job.

# Chapter 5
# DEVELOP A SPENDING PLAN

S EVERAL YEARS AGO *Saturday Night Live* aired a skit about budgeting. It boiled down to six simple words: "Don't buy stuff you cannot afford." The actors in the sketch could not grasp this simple concept, and it was both funny and sad to see them fail to understand that the way to get and stay out of debt was to not spend money they didn't have.

Unfortunately this is still true for many people, including those in the church. In my counseling and research, I've met many people who don't have a clue about living on a plan for spending and managing their money. There's another name for this much-needed spending plan. It's called a *budget*.

Budgeting can seem mundane and boring—and frustrating and very restrictive. Personally, I really don't like the term "budget." It makes me think of a diet or some form of medieval torture to punish past sins. But when we begin to see how a spending plan can help us achieve our financial goals, budgeting becomes exciting and life-giving.

Did Jesus have a spending plan? The Bible doesn't speak clearly on this subject, but I think so. There's nothing conclusive in Scripture, but we could say He held money management and the idea of planned spending in high regard. He had a treasurer of a sort: Judas. That didn't work out too well, of course, but He did assign the role.

In Luke 14, Jesus taught the concept of planned spending

as He encouraged people to be intentional about choosing to follow Him.

> For who among you, intending to build a tower, does not sit down first and count the cost to see whether he has resources to complete it? Otherwise, perhaps, after he has laid the foundation and is not able to complete it, all who see it will begin to mock him, saying, "This man began to build and was not able to complete it."
> —Luke 14:28–30, mev

God has said a lot in Scripture about planned spending and life planning in general. Budgeting is nothing more than spending money in an intentional way. To do something intentionally means you do it with purpose and according to a plan. Simply put, every dollar needs an assignment, or a job.

Even if you've never planned your finances before, chances are you have planned something in your lifetime. We plan our days often without even realizing it. We take our twenty-four hours and allocate it to things like sleep, work, chores around the house, or activities with the kids. We plan our vacations and how we're going to spend the holidays. We plan how to do our grocery run most efficiently so we don't waste time. I never go to the grocery store without a list of some kind— simply so I do not forget something. Ever forget to pay a bill because you didn't have it on your to-do list?

Perhaps you use a calendar pinned to the wall or on your smartphone or tablet. Perhaps you make notes to remind yourself of appointments or errands you need to run. Or maybe you set your clock so you'll get up in time to exercise or have your morning devotional. If you do any of those things, you're spending your day according to a plan.

If we plan our time, why shouldn't we plan how we're going to use our income? The Bible has a lot to say about planning.

God's heart is to bring order out of chaos. Isn't that what He did in the beginning at creation? The Bible goes on to tell us:

> The plans of the heart belong to man but the answer of the tongue is from the LORD. All the ways of man are pure in his own eyes, but the LORD weighs the spirit. Commit your work to the LORD, and your plans will be established.
>
> —PROVERBS 16:1–3, ESV

> The heart of man plans his way, but the LORD establishes his steps.
>
> —PROVERBS 16:9, ESV

> The plans of the diligent lead surely to abundance, but everyone who is hasty comes only to poverty.
>
> —PROVERBS 21:5, ESV

We really need to slow life down and make some plans. On a Saturday recently, I visited a car dealership, and before the sales rep and I even talked business, he wanted me to sign a document that said I would buy a car that day if we came to terms. I would not sign it. It was all I could do to not be rude and walk out!

Another time, my wife and I were checking out a gym membership. The salesman put us in a room and said the manager would be in to talk to us about special deals the facility was offering. The room was freezing cold. After what felt like an hour, the manager finally came in. He rattled off a series of deals, but by his attitude we could tell we would have to take advantage of those deals that day or they would be off the table forever. I thought, "Dude, my wife is about to take you out."

High-pressure tactics like these are used to get us to buy now. And too often this kind of pressure leads to bad decisions.

Always take the time to pray and seek God's guidance. And be ready to walk away from the deal. Scripture says,

> For the eyes of the LORD move about on all the earth to strengthen the heart that is completely toward Him.
> —2 CHRONICLES 16:9, MEV

God is waiting for us to pause—to take a break—so He can get into our circumstances and do something on our behalf. If we are diligent in planning and slow in decision making, we create space for Him to work.

Another good scripture on planning is Luke 16:10–11:

> Whoever can be trusted with very little can also be trusted with much, and whoever is dishonest with very little will also be dishonest with much. So if you have not been trustworthy in handling worldly wealth, who will trust you with true riches?
> —NIV

This works both for ministry and money. If you're faithful with little, you'll be faithful with much. And God will reward you.

## THE IDEAL VS. THE REAL

We live in constant tension between the *ideal* and the *real*. We know where we want to go. That's the *ideal*. But the tension between where we are and where we want to be can become so great we give up. We say, "I'll never achieve what I want to accomplish financially. So why bother? It's hopeless." Or we look at the *real* in our lives right now and say, "I'm never going to look the way I want to look, so pass me the bag of Oreos."

I live in this world too. My ideal includes items such as:

- I want my home paid off.

- I want to have the entire Bible memorized.

- I want a perfect body.

- I want to be super-fast on my bicycle.

- I want to preach like Gateway Church's senior
  pastor, Robert Morris, and manage like our
  senior executive pastor, Tom Lane!

My financial ideal is to live on one-third of our income, save one-third, and give one-third. And I want to be on Step 7 of the Route 7 Road Map. But the reality is that I do have a mortgage; my body is "almost perfect," according to my wife; and we are still working to reach our ideal financial situation.

I'm not where I want to be but, praise God, I'm not where I once was. God isn't finished with me yet. And He isn't finished with you either.

To get from where we are today (the real) to where we want to be (the ideal) takes a plan. It's not going to happen simply by wishing. It takes figuring out what we need to do to get where we want to be.

In chapter 8 we'll discuss life stewardship and take on life planning. But in this chapter, I want to focus on the basics of financial planning.

## Financial Planning 101

When it comes to financial planning, people often get frustrated when their income doesn't match their outgo. They may give up and hope to just have enough money to make it to the weekend or their next paycheck. Long-term planning goes out the window.

Let me encourage you. You *are* going to make it. It's all

about taking baby steps and making incremental changes to create a budget—a spending plan—you can actually live on. The decisions you make today will dictate where you end up tomorrow. This section on budgeting will help you make the wisest decisions to meet your goals.

While I was working in construction, I started a process of learning scriptures. I wanted to know where all the verses about money were located, and I wanted to memorize them. Years later I connected this practice to my calling to be a pastor. I realized I would eventually teach and counsel people from these very scriptures. God did this again and again, showing me how one step led to another that would take me exactly where I was supposed to be. My willingness to make plans that took me in the direction God was leading gave Him the opportunity to work.

Whether you make ten thousand dollars a year or over a million, it's all the same—you have to plan how you will spend your money.

There are some definite pros to having a spending plan.

### An unexpected raise

For one thing, you'll give yourself about a 20 percent pay raise when you carefully watch and manage your money. One man at my church told me he figured he would save over three hundred dollars a month if he brought his lunch from home instead of eating out with colleagues. As you pay attention, you'll find other little things that could add up to substantial savings. Make your coffee at home and save all that money spent at "Bigbucks."

### Better communication

Living on a spending plan will help you better communicate with your spouse. When you're planning the household spending, you have to talk things through. When this happens, you end up on the same page and your household runs more smoothly. For my wife and me, money was our worst area of communication. We fought like cats and dogs over our finances. Today it's our best area of communication. We do not mind sitting down, going over our finances, and planning what we need to do and what little tweaks we need to make to achieve our goals. Usually we each are able to buy items we have wanted because, working together, we see the money is there.

Managing finances also will highlight communication breakdowns. I see this happening among the departments at my church as budget discussions take place. Just like in a marriage, we see where people have been acting on assumptions because there hadn't been clear communication. A budget is a litmus test for how well you communicate.

### Less stress

There is much less financial stress when you plan your spending. When you allocate your money, giving each dollar a job, you're not worrying about using grocery money to pay your electric bill.

### Debt elimination

As you put your plan together and follow it, your debt will start to shrink. Make no mistake, it will be a process that takes time, but believe me, you will eventually get out of debt.

### Increased giving

When you plan spending, you will see where you have room to increase your giving because you have a firmer handle on your finances.

### Financial surplus

With a spending plan, you will create more margin in your life. You'll gradually build a surplus and reach the point where you won't live paycheck-to-paycheck.

**Achieved goals**

You will eventually reach your financial goals.

**Reduced impulse buying**

Having a budget will cause you to slow down your spending decisions. A spending plan quashes impulse buying because you have to look at the numbers. For example, my wife and I spent three months shopping for her car after deciding on the year, make, and model before we found the one that fit our spending plan. Being patient saved us over five thousand dollars. In my household, that is worth the wait!

## TODAY'S PLAN DETERMINES TOMORROW'S DIRECTION

Effective budgeting will require discipline in your life, because your lifestyle will change as you live by a budget. For example, when we committed to budgeting, I stopped visiting Dunkin' Donuts every morning. I switched to making coffee at home— and I hate making coffee, especially cleaning out the used grounds. But I made the change because I could see the value in it for our finances and our family.

What determines how intensely you budget? *Don't miss this.* It is determined by where you are in your calling. Your lifestyle decisions determine not only the direction you'll go, but also how intensely you'll pursue any changes you need to make to meet your goals.

When I was in construction, I was in good shape financially but I was not walking in my calling to pastor. I needed to be gung ho about my financial plan at that time. If I hadn't been—if I hadn't purposely and enthusiastically adjusted my lifestyle to reduce our expenses despite having a strong income—I would not have been able to move into full-time ministry when God called me to do so.

In chapter 4, we talked about the four groups of people in

the world: those who are walking in their calling and are in good shape financially, those who are walking in their calling and are in bad shape financially, those who are in good shape financially but aren't walking in their calling, and those who are in bad shape financially and aren't walking in their calling.

If you're walking in your calling and are in good shape financially, that's great. Steady as you go.

If you're walking in your calling but are *not* in good shape financially, that's OK too. Keep reading. This book can help fix that.

If you're not walking in your calling but are in good shape financially, we can help with that as well. Not too long ago, I began counseling a recently retired businessman. He was in great shape financially but didn't know how he should serve God during that season in his life. We began working together to help him find where God wanted him to be, and the journey to discover his calling has given him more inspiration than any hobby he ever enjoyed.

If you're not walking in your calling and are in bad shape financially, you're in a tough place. Here are three possible explanations for why you find yourself in this position. I could write a book on this alone, so I will only give you the highlights here.

## 1. Wrong attitude

Having a wrong attitude is like putting the incorrect address in a GPS system. No matter how hard we try to do the right things in our relationship with money, if we have greed, covetousness, deception, dishonesty, arrogance, pride, envy, fear, indulgence, or pride giving us directions, we will end up in pain or trouble. The Bible tells us this again and again.

> The *greedy* stir up conflict, but those who trust in the
> LORD will prosper.
>
> —PROVERBS 28:25, NIV, EMPHASIS ADDED

> For the love of money is a root of all kinds of evil, for
> which some have strayed from the faith in their greed-
> iness, and pierced themselves through with many
> sorrows.
>
> —1 TIMOTHY 6:10

## 2. Bad management

Not managing our life calling and our finances well will
lead to complete frustration. To break this cycle, I recommend
concentrating on two areas. First, get alone with God and
ask Him what He has called you to do. Then write down the
impressions that come to your heart and see if you can find
biblical references for those impressions. After you've spent
time with the Lord, seek counsel from trusted friends and
apply the lesson in chapter 8 on life stewardship.

Once you've sought the Lord and trusted counsel about your
calling in life, begin to live by a spending plan. You may even
want to get a financial coach who will hold you accountable.
(Many local churches as well as Compass financial ministry
and Dave Ramsey offer recommendations on their websites.)
If your finances are a mess, developing a clear spending plan
will show you why. No guessing anymore. When you can pin-
point the problem areas, you can then make wise decisions
based on facts, not guesswork. Scripture encourages us to be
diligent and not just let things happen:

> Slothfulness casts into a deep sleep, and an idle soul will
> suffer hunger.
>
> —PROVERBS 19:15, MEV

> Do not love sleep or you will grow poor; stay awake and
> you will have food to spare.
>                                          —PROVERBS 20:13, NIV

### 3. Course adjustment

Sometimes our finances and our sense of calling may be
in disarray through no fault of our own. We all go through
rough times, and by no means do I desire to be one of Job's bad
friends who blamed him for his misfortune. Even in the dark
times God is showing us things and possibly even training us to
lead new ministry efforts. He may be using those circumstances
to redirect our course. Keep your ears open and your head on
straight, and get involved in a good church. You will make it
through this season.

Whatever group you fall into, the important thing is to
keep the big picture—your *ideal*—in front of you and to take
a balanced approach to budgeting. I see people who are so set
on their goals that they neglect other areas of their lives, and
they suffer all kinds of negative consequences. I've counseled
families who went crazy intense on their financial plan only
to have major marital problems as a result of their over-the-
top approach. A divorce destroys more than the financial plan.

I've seen couples stop having date nights because they were
so focused on meeting their financial goals. They worked
so many hours they didn't even see each other—they didn't
have time! If you're working two or three jobs to meet certain
financial goals, you're losing time with your spouse and your
kids, and you could be putting your health at risk. Is meeting
your financial or life goal really worth divorce or death? Bring
some balance to your plan. A short season of ultra-intensity is
good for you, but don't live there long-term.

Be really careful about putting your family in an unsafe
$500 beater car just to get out of debt. Their safety is worth so
much more than debt freedom. As a man who is good with

wrenches, I have done the beater car for myself, but I would never do that to my wife and children in the Dallas/Fort Worth area. Intensity is good, but keep it all in perspective.

One of the most important things to remember is not to break the Sabbath rest principle, even if you have a fantastic plan. This is a violation of the Ten Commandments and it's just plain bad for you. I don't care how good your plan looks, working a hundred hours a week will cost you much more than you could ever gain. God wants us to rest and even modeled it at creation because our bodies were designed to *need* rest. We can't go nonstop, no matter what our goals.

The Lord had to deal with me in this area. I was a workaholic, working seven days a week and wondering why there weren't more hours in the day. Under His urging, I cut back to working six days a week, then five. Working only five days a week in construction was unheard of in South Florida. Then God told me to cut back to four days a week and give one day to the church, serving in any capacity they asked me to.

"Lord," I said. "That's crazy. I can't run a construction company four days a week. If I'm not there, there will be mayhem. I have projects lined up. I can't do this."

But God said, "Do you trust Me?"

How do you say argue with that? In obedience to God's direction, I met with my pastor, and he asked that I spend Thursdays counseling and doing Crown Ministries business.

I explained my schedule to the contractors I worked for. Sunday was dedicated to church, Saturday to my family, and Thursday to serving the church. The contractors paid me more to keep their projects a priority and to drop other builders. Looking back, I made more money being obedient to God and working four days a week than I ever did working seven.

I could feel God nudging me with His elbow. "Didn't I tell you? My ways are better than your ways."

Remember Proverbs 3:5–6:

> Trust in the Lord with all your heart, and lean not on your own understanding; in all your ways acknowledge Him, and He shall direct your paths.

## The Jesus Model for Financial Planning

At the end of the day, our financial plans aren't that big of a deal. Yes, it is wise to seek God's wisdom and to exercise foresight in managing money, setting goals and targets, and aiming for them. But the big deal is, did I do the will of my Father? Will I hear Him say, "Well done, good and faithful servant"? When it's all said and done, all our plans, whether financial or career or ministry, should result in our walking in God's plans for us.

Jesus describes this for us in John 6:38:

> For I have come down from heaven, not to do My own will, but the will of Him who sent Me.

His instruction to us makes this clear.

> Therefore pray in this manner: Our Father who is in heaven, hallowed be Your name. Your kingdom come; *Your will be done* on earth, as it is in heaven.
> —Matthew 6:9–10, mev, emphasis added

Jesus's model was to do the Father's will, not His own will. This needs to be our priority as well: His will, not ours. We need to make the time to get alone with God and seek His will and His plan for our lives. Ask Him, "God, what is Your will for my life? What am I supposed to do? Where am I supposed to go?"

Scripture shows us that Jesus, who was God's Son, did this very thing when He walked the earth.

> He withdrew from them about a stone's throw, and He knelt down and prayed, "Father, if You are willing, remove this cup from Me. Nevertheless not My will, but Yours, be done."
>
> —LUKE 22:41–42, MEV

If Jesus sought the Lord for His will, how much more should we?

The trump card in all planning is, "Lord, what do You want me to do? Where do I live? Do we buy this house? Do I take this job? Do we put our kids in home school, private school, or public school?"

Wrestle with all these questions before the Lord. Listen for His voice. And follow His leading, even if that means delaying eliminating debt and reaching your financial goals.

| Route 7 Road Map Step 3 |
| --- |
| ■ Increase giving percentage. |
| ■ Pay off all loans. |
| ■ Increase emergency fund to three months of living expenses. |

## YOUR ROUTE 7 ACTION PLAN

You may have created a spending plan in the past and drifted away from it, or you may be following one now. Either way, at this point in the journey I'd encourage you to take inventory of where you are in your financial planning and where you want to go.

Planning is a fluid process. We're constantly learning new things, and we're constantly seeing the effect of changes we

are making and adjusting for those. We review to make sure
we haven't missed anything and that we're still on track.

So at this point in the process, get together with your spouse
and discuss and write down your goals. The first time Missy
and I did this, it felt a little silly to be asking my wife what her
financial goals and dreams were. We had that uncomfortable
feeling you get when you're doing something for the first time.
I'm glad we pushed past that discomfort. We hit pay dirt as we
shared our dreams and desires. Communication opened up,
and the list we created helped guide our decision making as the
years went along.

Not too long ago I was discussing this with a friend, helping
him process the concepts I've been sharing. I asked him, "What
is God doing in your life? How much is enough? Where are you
going in your walk with the Lord?"

He answered, "I can't grow my business any larger and still
do what God's called me to do. If I expand, I may make a little
more money, but I'll lose the time I have to work for Him. It
isn't worth it."

Nine months later he called me. "I have this phenomenal
opportunity to expand my business."

"Let me ask a question," I said. "What's changed in your
goals, in the plans we discussed a few months ago?"

He hesitated. "That's a good question. You know, my wife
and I have both had nagging feelings about this move. She
more than me, but you've confirmed what's been stirring in us.
We're not going to go down that path. I'm not going to expand
my business."

Setting goals and writing them down is so helpful in
keeping us focused. To paraphrase Habakkuk 2:2, "Write the
vision." If you don't have it written down, how will you know
what to aim for or when you've achieved it?

After you've set your goals, determine your income. Figure out exactly how much you're bringing in.

Now plan your spending for the month, but allocate by pay period using whatever tools work best for you. It could be the envelope method, YNAB (youneedabudget.com), MINT (mint.com), Quicken, spreadsheets, or a combination of several tools—whatever gives you the best overview of both your income and your obligations. Then budget according to your pay period.

If you get paid every two weeks rather than twice a month, base your budget on two paychecks. Look at the math. If you get paid twice a month, you collect twenty-four checks in a year. If you get paid every two weeks, you get twenty-six checks. This is like an extra month's pay. It's a bonus. Don't spend it on everyday stuff. Earmark these extra checks for savings, building up your emergency fund, or for getting out of debt. If you're self-employed, you have to pay attention to the expense side of your budget so you'll know how much income you need to bring in.

Finally, at the end of the month, go back and balance your budget. See what happened to your money and make adjustments. YNAB, MINT, and even bank websites all have tools to help do this.

Ministries such as Dave Ramsey (daveramsey.com), Crown Ministries (crown.org), and Compass Ministry (compass1.org) also have excellent guidelines and charts to show how to allocate our income by percentage. The following chart is just one example. Remember, these are recommendations. Your percentages don't have to match what they suggest, but it is very helpful to allocate your income by percentage.

| MONTHLY SPENDING PLAN | | | | | |
|---|---|---|---|---|---|
| Categories | Actual From Register | % of Gross Income | Guideline % | Guideline Amount | Budget Amount |
| **Net income** | | | | | |
| **Giving** (tithes, offerings) | | | | | |
| **Food** | | | | | |
| Groceries | | | | | |
| Restau-rants | | | | | |
| **Housing** | | | | | |
| Mortgage/ rent | | | | | |
| Electricity/ gas | | | | | |
| Water | | | | | |
| Telephone/ cell Phone | | | | | |
| Internet/ TV Service | | | | | |
| Mainte-nance and repairs | | | | | |
| House/ rental insurance | | | | | |
| Taxes | | | | | |
| Other | | | | | |

| MONTHLY SPENDING PLAN | | | | | |
|---|---|---|---|---|---|
| Categories | Actual From Register | % of Gross Income | Guideline % | Guideline Amount | Budget Amount |
| **Miscellaneous** | | | | | |
| Gifts | | | | | |
| Other | | | | | |
| **Personal** | | | | | |
| Health/ life/ disability premiums | | | | | |
| Health out-of-pocket expenses | | | | | |
| Flexible spending account | | | | | |
| Hair care | | | | | |
| Clothing | | | | | |
| **Recreation** | | | | | |
| His | | | | | |
| Hers | | | | | |
| Entertain-ment | | | | | |
| Vacation | | | | | |

| MONTHLY SPENDING PLAN | | | | | |
|---|---|---|---|---|---|
| Categories | Actual From Register | % of Gross Income | Guideline % | Guideline Amount | Budget Amount |
| **Transportation** | | | | | |
| Car payment | | | | | |
| Gas | | | | | |
| Car insurance | | | | | |
| License/ registration | | | | | |
| Maintenance and repairs | | | | | |
| **Savings** | | | | | |
| **Child expenses** (tuition, lessons, day care) | | | | | |
| **Debt** (credit card, student loans, etc.) | | | | | |
| **Net income — Expenses** | | | | | |

## SPENDING GUIDELINES

### PERCENTAGES OF NET INCOME

| Category | Single w/o Roommate | | Single w/Roommate | | Singe Parent | | |
|---|---|---|---|---|---|---|---|
| | $23,000 | $32,000 | $23,000 | $32,000 | $15,000 | $20,000 | $25,000 |
| Giving | 13% | 13% | 13% | 13% | 10% | 11% | 11% |
| Food | 5% | 5% | 5% | 5% | 13% | 13% | 13% |
| Housing | 35% | 34% | 24% | 24% | 37% | 35% | 33% |
| Miscellaneous | 5% | 6% | 5% | 7% | 4% | 4% | 5% |
| Personal | 13% | 11% | 13% | 11% | 12% | 12% | 12% |
| Recreation | 7% | 6% | 10% | 10% | 4% | 4% | 3% |
| Transportation | 16% | 16% | 17% | 17% | 13% | 13% | 13% |
| Savings | 6% | 9% | 13% | 13% | 4% | 4% | 5% |
| Child Expenses | 0% | 0% | 0% | 0% | 3% | 4% | 5% |
| Total | 100% | 100% | 100% | 100% | 100% | 100% | 100% |

## SPENDING GUIDELINES

### *PERCENTAGES OF NET INCOME*

| Category | Married Couple | | | | | | |
|---|---|---|---|---|---|---|---|
| | $15,000 | $25,000 | $35,000 | $45,000 | $55,000 | $65,000 | $115,000 |
| Giving | 11% | 12% | 12% | 13% | 13% | 13% | 14% |
| Food | 14% | 11% | 11% | 10% | 10% | 10% | 10% |
| Housing | 35% | 32% | 29% | 27% | 26% | 26% | 24% |
| Miscellaneous | 4% | 5% | 6% | 6% | 7% | 7% | 6% |
| Personal | 12% | 12% | 12% | 13% | 13% | 13% | 14% |
| Recreation | 3% | 4% | 5% | 6% | 6% | 7% | 7% |
| Transportation | 14% | 13% | 13% | 12% | 12% | 11% | 10% |
| Savings | 7% | 11% | 12% | 13% | 13% | 13% | 15% |
| Child Expenses | 0% | 0% | 0% | 0% | 0% | 0% | 0% |
| Total | 100% | 100% | 100% | 100% | 100% | 100% | 100% |

## SPENDING GUIDELINES

### PERCENTAGES OF NET INCOME

| Category | Family of Four | | | | | | | | |
|---|---|---|---|---|---|---|---|---|---|
| | $25,000 | $35,000 | $45,000 | $55,000 | $65,000 | $85,000 | $115,000 | | |
| Giving | 10% | 11% | 12% | 12% | 12% | 13% | 14% | | |
| Food | 13% | 12% | 11% | 11% | 10% | 9% | 9% | | |
| Housing | 35% | 31% | 28% | 27% | 26% | 26% | 26% | | |
| Miscellaneous | 3% | 4% | 5% | 5% | 5% | 5% | 5% | | |
| Personal | 12% | 13% | 14% | 14% | 15% | 15% | 15% | | |
| Recreation | 4% | 4% | 5% | 6% | 6% | 7% | 7% | | |
| Transportation | 14% | 13% | 12% | 12% | 12% | 12% | 11% | | |
| Savings | 4% | 7% | 8% | 8% | 9% | 9% | 9% | | |
| Child Expenses | 5% | 5% | 5% | 5% | 5% | 4% | 4% | | |
| Total | 100% | 100% | 100% | 100% | 100% | 100% | 100% | | |

## SPENDING GUIDELINES

### PERCENTAGES OF NET INCOME

| Category | $25,000 | $35,000 | $45,000 | Family of Six $55,000 | $65,000 | $85,000 | $115,000 |
|---|---|---|---|---|---|---|---|
| Giving | 10% | 11% | 11% | 12% | 12% | 13% | 13% |
| Food | 13% | 13% | 13% | 12% | 12% | 11% | 10% |
| Housing | 35% | 34% | 31% | 29% | 29% | 29% | 29% |
| Miscellaneous | 4% | 5% | 6% | 6% | 5% | 5% | 5% |
| Personal | 13% | 13% | 13% | 14% | 15% | 16% | 17% |
| Recreation | 4% | 4% | 4% | 5% | 5% | 5% | 5% |
| Transportation | 13% | 12% | 11% | 10% | 10% | 9% | 8% |
| Savings | 4% | 4% | 7% | 7% | 7% | 8% | 9% |
| Child Expenses | 4% | 4% | 4% | 5% | 5% | 4% | 4% |
| Total | 100% | 100% | 100% | 100% | 100% | 100% | 100% |

Seeing how well your spending matches the percentage guidelines can help you quickly determine if some area of your budget is out of whack. Here is a case in point. A couple came in to see me for counseling, and one of the first things they said was, "We love our house." The problem was since they'd bought it three years earlier, they had run up $36,000 in credit card debt. Of course, the first expense I looked at was the house. In 2007, they had taken out a $550,000 variable rate, interest-only mortgage without escrowing property taxes or insurance. They earned $60,000 per year. They got into the house by taking a non-qualifying loan and using an inheritance check as a down payment. The mortgage lender did not verify their income.

Every month, they were short at least $2,500 dollars.

I used a percentage chart to show them that 74 percent of their spendable income was being devoted to their house. Simply put, they had a house they couldn't afford.

I was prepared to play the bad guy, but as we reviewed the numbers and the percentages, they came to the realization on their own. They were in way over their heads with too much house for their income. All on their own, they decided to sell.

When looking at percentage guidelines, like the ones in the previous chart, don't see them as rigid, never-to-be-violated rules. You can be over in some areas and under in others to balance everything out. For example, some people eat out a lot and spend way over the recommended percentage for food. But their house is paid off, so the percentage of their income that goes toward housing is much less than the guideline suggests.

After you've figured out how to use the percentages to their best advantage, align your goals with the Route 7 objectives and with your calling. If you're not in that sweet spot where you are flexible enough financially to pursue the things God is calling you to do, look at your numbers and figure out how to increase your margin. Once you've created enough margin, when the opportunity arises, you'll be in a position to move into that new area God has planned for you.

If your income is less than your budget, you need to get creative in your planning. Remember the three options we outlined earlier: make more money, spend less money, or sell stuff. As I noted, spending less is the most effective option for getting a budget into balance. And here's another preemptive strategy: don't buy stuff you cannot afford.

## MANAGING SPENDING DURING FINANCIAL CRISIS

What if you're in a financial crisis? For several years I oversaw the benevolence fund at our church and daily dealt with people in crisis. Through that experience I learned that if you're in financial crisis, the first thing to do is stop and pray.

One day a single mother came to see me. Her husband had taken a job as a street-side pharmaceutical supplier—he was dealing drugs. He was arrested, and in Florida when you're arrested on drug charges you lose your car immediately. Sadly they were a one-car family. The husband was a multiple offender, and this was his third strike, so he was facing a mandatory ten-year sentence.

After this woman shared her situation with me, I told her we had to pray. She looked at me like I was crazy. But I told her we needed God's wisdom to help get her out of that situation. As we prayed that God would provide a car for her family, I could tell she didn't really believe me, but I used my faith to stand in the gap for her. Almost immediately after we met, the woman received a phone call from her mother. She had used her income tax refund to buy her daughter a car and was driving it down from Michigan. Praise the Lord!

The next thing to do after you pray is get counsel. When we're in a crisis, we tend to get tunnel vision. We don't see the whole picture, and our focus may not be where it should be. Counseling will help you see different viewpoints and give you new ideas. Plus, counseling helps you connect with a bigger group of people. As you hear more perspectives, more options will open up. I've seen crises resolved in life groups because of the connections that are made in those small settings.

Third, when you're in crisis, plan your financial moves very, very carefully. Meet your basic needs for food, transportation, and housing first. Then live on a shoestring budget with the rest of the money, stretching it as far as it will go. Be creative, and be ready to make hard decisions.

Notice I didn't include debt in my list of basic needs. If you're in crisis, I don't want you paying a MasterCard bill if you don't have enough food for your family. First Timothy 5:8 tells us that those who don't take care of their families are worse than unbelievers.

Finally when you're walking through a crisis, over-communicate with your creditors. Keep in touch with them regularly. When you initiate contact and explain your difficulties, they frequently don't know what to do with you. They're used to people running away from them. You're coming to them. They're more likely to be cooperative when this happens.

I also recommend you use Dave Ramsey's Pro Rata Plan. Pro Rata means "Fair Share." On your shoestring budget, take what you have left after you've met your basic necessities and use it to pay a creditor. Divide it up based on the percentage you owe each creditor and send it out. It won't be a full payment, but it will be something. By doing this, you're acknowledging that you know you need to pay off your debts. Even though you may not be making as much progress toward eliminating the debt as you'd like, and even if you're not paying the minimum balance, making these small payments will buy you some time until you're on your feet again and can fully meet your obligations.

When you follow this strategy, pay your secured debts such as your mortgage first. Then pay your unsecured debt such as your credit cards. These unsecured debt holders will call you quickly and can be nasty and ugly. This is why it works best to contact them first and stay in communication so they will know you're not ignoring your debt.

There's a book called *Money Troubles* put out by an organization called NOLO, which means "Law for All." It has some suggested form letters to use when communicating with creditors. Dave Ramsey also has similar letters on his website.

## MANAGING CAR DEBT

One of the keys to being successful in following the Route 7 Road Map is to get out of automobile debt and stay out. This process will take time, but it is so worth it. Here are five steps to conquer the car debt monster.

1. Keep your car for three years after the loan is paid off. If you have a four-year note on your car, plan on keeping it seven years—at least.

2. Include the car payment in your debt-elimination snowball plan (we will discuss that at length in chapter 7), and knock it out as quickly as you can.

3. After the car is paid off, continue to make the car payments, only pay them to yourself, not the creditor. Set them aside in a separate "new car" account so you won't be tempted to spend them on a big-screen TV.

4. Use this saved cash plus your car to purchase a newer used car.

5. Repeat the process of saving and upgrading. Keep making the car payment to yourself and saving it, and soon you'll be paying cash for an excellent used car.

## Depreciation: Value vs. Cost

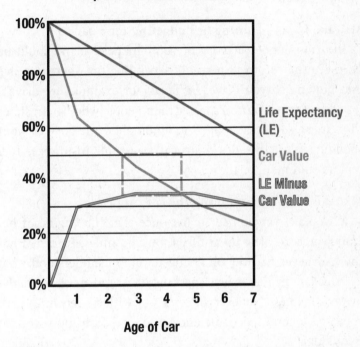

**Age of Car**

We want our cars to maintain the maximum value for the longest amount of time. This plan will get us there and keep us there.

It's not always wrong to buy a brand-new car, but because of rapid depreciation, it's seldom wise. If you want to buy a brand-new car, I suggest you plan on driving it at least ten years so you can recoup your cost.

Today's cars will last fifteen to twenty years. But we pay for them at the beginning, and then they depreciate. If we drive the car for only five years or less, we've lost a lot of the value of that car. On average, a person drives a new car for around six to eight years, so as you can see, most people don't get their money's worth out of a car.[1]

In my counseling experiences, I've discovered a lot of mistakes people make with their cars. Below are the top ten car mistakes people make.

### Mistake 1: Not planning or budgeting for a car

The automobile category of your financial plan should be no more than 15 to 18 percent, depending on where you live and how much you drive. In Texas, for example, we drive a lot and wear out our cars faster than people who live in states that aren't so spread out. The automobile category of your spending plan includes your car payment, insurance, fuel, repairs, and maintenance.

### Mistake 2: Not maintaining the car properly

A woman complained to me once that the engine of her Honda Accord blew up at fifty thousand miles. It turned out she had never had the oil changed. She misunderstood what the dealer told her when she bought it and never read the owner's manual. Not everyone is savvy with a wrench. If that's you, find a good mechanic and build a relationship with that individual.

### Mistake 3: Buying the wrong car for their situation

I had a friend who bought an expensive two-seat sports car right after getting married. Three months later, his wife was pregnant, and the car had to go.

Another friend bought a Dodge Hemi truck that he loved. He lived in Fort Worth and worked in North Dallas, which made his commute around one hundred miles per day. The truck got ten miles per gallon. The cost of gas alone was eating up his income. He would have been better off buying a Toyota Corolla and slapping a Hemi decal on the side of it.

### Mistake 4: Not getting a prepurchase inspection by their mechanic

One time Missy and I found a Suburban we liked. It met our wish list to the letter. Before we purchased it, I took it to my mechanic for an inspection. He told us not to buy the vehicle. The frame was rusted out and had been sandblasted and repainted to disguise the damage, and he was concerned the car would fold up like a cardboard box in a wreck. I'm not telling you to distrust all car salesmen, but I like to follow the advice Ronald Reagan once gave: trust, but verify.

### Mistake 5: Letting the car dealer bully them

I'm sure you've experienced car salesmen who put you in a little room while they go talk with the sales manager about the deal because "he's got the numbers." Don't let them play these games. Follow the salesman into the manager's office and tell him or her, "Here's what I want to pay. Call me when you're ready to talk numbers." Then I'm out the door.

### Mistake 6: Getting bad financing

Avoid getting financing through the dealer. Your objective is to get the car paid off without paying a ton of interest. That means you want to get the lowest interest rate you can for the shortest term you can afford and pay it off early.

I recommend you get your own financing through a local credit union. Several years ago, I went to a dealer to buy a "new" used car. I found the right car, and the finance office wanted to charge me 20 percent interest because of my credit score (which was in the high 700s, by the way!). I went to another dealer and bought the same exact car at 4 percent interest.

## Mistake 7: Cosigning

*Never, never, never, ever* cosign a loan for anyone, especially family. Cosigning is backing someone else's credit. And if they had any credit, they wouldn't need a cosigner. Don't cosign for your children. Let them drive something a little older. Let them put some skin in the game and really work at this thing. Scripture backs this up.

> One who lacks sense gives a pledge and puts up security in the presence of his neighbor.
> —Proverbs 17:18, esv

> Be not one of those who give pledges, who put up security for debts. If you have nothing with which to pay, why should your bed be taken from under you?
> —Proverbs 22:26–27, esv

> Whoever puts up security for a stranger will surely suffer harm, but he who hates striking hands in pledge is secure.
> —Proverbs 11:15, esv

If you've already cosigned a loan, get out of it! Look at what Proverbs 6:1–5 says:

> My son, if you have put up security for your neighbor, have given your pledge for a stranger, if you are snared in the words of your mouth, caught in the words of your mouth, then do this, my son, and save yourself, for you have come into the hand of your neighbor: go, hasten, and plead urgently with your neighbor. Give your eyes no sleep and your eyelids no slumber; save yourself like a gazelle from the hand of the hunter, like a bird from the hand of the fowler.
> —esv

I paraphrase it this way: Go nuts until you can get out of that cosigning deal. If you can't give the person the car, don't cosign.

### Mistake 8: Selling too soon or too late

My goal is to drive a car as economically as possible, at between five cents and twenty-five cents per mile. I have a simplified formula that helps me calculate the cost per mile. I take the purchase price of the car, add the maintenance and repair expenses (not gas or insurance), subtract what I sell the old car for, then divide that figure by the number of miles I drove the old car.

The formula looks something like this:

> New Car Purchase Price + Maintenance & Repairs – Estimated Sales Price of Old Car ÷ Miles Driven on Old Car = Cost Per Mile

To put this in real numbers, let's say you see a car that costs $10,700. It will cost roughly $1,400 to repair and maintain. You can sell your old car for $9,500, and you've driven it 25,000 miles. So if we apply our formula, we'd get:

$10,700 + $1,400 = $12,100

$12,100 – $9,500 = $2,600

$2,600 ÷ 25,000 = .104

So in this example, the cost per mile is .104. That looks like a good deal to me.

### Mistake 9: Falling into the leasing trap

Most of the time leasing is a very expensive way, if not *the* most expensive way, to drive a car. When you lease, you pay for the depreciation over and over again. Dealers like it because not only do they profit from your lease payments, but when the lease is over they have a very nice, well-maintained car for their used-car market. And they can sell it for a higher price than a non-leased car.

There is only one exception to this rule: electric cars. Several factors change the affordability of a lease on an electric car. First, at the time of this writing, there are federal and some state incentives that pay for as much as one-third of the car on a lease. If purchased the buyer must owe a minimum of $7,500 in personal income taxes to claim the full rebate.

Electric cars also do not require gasoline, oil changes, and other maintenance besides tire rotations, making them much cheaper to operate. A third factor that makes leasing an electric car more desirable than purchasing one is the technology is new and quickly changing. This causes the electric car to decrease in value rapidly, making leasing more economical.

However, electric cars are not for everyone due to their limited range. Make sure you check with your accountant and carefully assess your driving situation to see if this would be a wise option. For our family, leasing our Nissan Leaf has been less expensive than any other car we've ever owned.

### Mistake 10: Buying the car without praying or talking with their spouse

Here's another simple formula for you:

No prayer + no peace + no unity = no purchase.

No matter how good the deal looks, if God hasn't released you to buy the vehicle, or if you and your wife are not on the same page about making the purchase, walk away.

As you implement your spending plan, you may find that you need to make adjustments. That's what Route 7 is all about, assessing what God wants you to do and developing a strategy to meet those goals. If you need to course correct or revise your budget, do it! That means you're allowing God to redirect you in the area of finances, and that's a good thing. My prayer for you is that you'll constantly seek God for His will and adjust your plans as needed.

Knowing where every dollar is going is an important foundation to have in place if you want to build up your savings and eliminate debt, which are the topics we'll discuss in the next two chapters.

# Chapter 6

# BUILDING A SAVINGS STOREHOUSE

HIS CHAPTER WAS a challenge for me to prepare. As I thought about this subject and started gathering information, I began to wrestle with several questions:

- Does saving show a lack of faith?

- Is it foolish not to save?

- How much should I save?

- How do I guard against hoarding and greed?

- With so many starving people in the world, how do I balance saving with giving and my need to live on the money God has given me?

Thankfully the longer I researched information for this chapter, the more God began to answer those questions for me. I believe as we explore the topic of saving on our generous life journey, He will answer those questions for you too.

## FINDING BALANCE

Recently I saw a chart that helped put wealth, poverty, needs, and wants into some into perspective for me. Consider these statistics.[1]

If the world were made up of one hundred people:

- Sixty-seven wouldn't know Jesus (thirty-three would).

- Sixty would be Asian, fifteen African, nine South American, five North American, and eleven European.

- Five would live in the United States or Canada.

- Fifty would be male and fifty would be female.

- Forty-eight would live on less than two dollars a day.

- Twenty-three would have no roof over their head.

- Seventeen would not be able to read.

- Fifteen would be malnourished, meaning they would not have enough food and the food they did have wouldn't provide proper nutrition.

- One would be dying of starvation as you read this.

- One would control 50 percent of the world's wealth.[2]

What if you were the dad of the kid who was dying of malnourishment? Wouldn't you be asking that wealthy person to spare a little for your child? Unfortunately, for those of us who live in wealthier nations, the answer all too often is, "We need to do other things with our money."

This response rings hollow when we look at how Americans actually spend their money.[3]

- Thirty-four percent is spent on housing.

- Seventeen percent is spent on transportation.

- Sixteen percent is spent on recreation and per-sonal needs—what we do for fun.

- Thirteen percent is spent on food.

- Ten percent is spent on life insurance and retire-ment contributions.

- Six percent is spent on health care (insur-ance, prescriptions, cold medicines, health club memberships).

- Four percent is put into savings.

Does that leave anything for the kid on the other side of the world who is dying? Non-Christians around the world give around 2 percent of their income to organizations that may make a difference in that kid's life. If you're a Christian, that number skyrockets all the way to 3 percent.

In the United States one of our national pastimes seems to be living above our means. Our government is deep in debt, and so are the American people. We spend an awful lot more than we bring in. Individuals and families are rapidly increasing their debt load because of the belief we don't have enough stuff. And many Americans are among those who have an abundance of resources.

When I look at the statistics, I can't help but think of the opportunity we as the church have for massive influence. But where do we begin? We begin by going to God and asking Him to help us find balance and set right priorities. We must ask for His perspective on saving, giving, and how to live a balanced life as we seek to bring rest and comfort to those who are despairing.

This weighs heavily on me at times, but I'm comforted knowing God is not caught off guard by the world's challenges.

Our questions won't catch Him by surprise either—He has put everything we need in Scripture.

The answer is neither forced socialism nor forced giving. The answer lies in people who are open to hearing from God and who choose to live generous lives in Christ. The Apostle Paul wrote, "For I have learned to be content whatever the circumstances. I know what it is to be in need, and I know what it is to have plenty. I have learned the secret of being content in any and every situation, whether well fed or hungry, whether living in plenty or in want. I can do all things through Christ who gives me strength" (Phil. 4:11–14). Contentment is key to finding and living a balanced life financially.

Before we go any further in exploring the issue of savings, would you join me in asking God to show us how to lead balanced lives financially and be content in Him?

> *Father, how do we balance saving, giving, and living? What does Your Scripture say to us as Christians in a blessed country about how to impact a hurting and dying world? Lord, please show us how to do this. Bless us as we search out Your Word and find wisdom in Your teaching. Holy Spirit, we invite You to be our Teacher. In Christ's name, amen.*

## ASCETICISM AND MATERIALISM

There are two sides to this coin we've been discussing. On one side is asceticism and on the other is materialism.

*Asceticism* is the side most of our forerunners in the faith leaned toward, and it continues in some circles even today. Curiously it may not have a solid biblical basis.

Asceticism describes a lifestyle characterized by abstinence from various worldly pleasures, often with the aim of pursuing religious and spiritual goals. The thinking is that a form of poverty creates holiness. Christian authors such as Origen, Jerome, and Augustine interpreted biblical texts within a highly ascetic religious environment.

My overly simplistic interpretation of some of what they taught is, "I'm going to deny myself to be closer to God." To be holy was to be absolutely poor, to shun material goods.

There are some well-meaning ministers today who teach asceticism—to get rid of all material possessions in our Christian life so we can be holy and pleasing to God. While studying this topic, I read a story about Mother Teresa. Her fellow missionaries received a gift that included a home to help people. The home had carpet, hot water, and other amenities— and the sisters took them all out. They turned off the hot water and removed the carpet because they had committed to an austere lifestyle and didn't want to enjoy any of those comforts. That was the lifestyle they felt was pleasing to God.[4]

When I began studying asceticism, my first thought was, "Lord, I'm just going to give everything away." I was comforted when He said to me, "Maybe that's not what I'm asking you to do. Maybe that's not what I'm asking you to teach."

Sometimes a person receives a revelation from the Lord for his own personal lifestyle, and he thinks it should be applied to everyone. Some things God tells us to do aren't meant for everyone; they're adjustments He wants us to make in our own lives.

The Bible provides guiding principles for how to live, but God didn't give us a checklist in Scripture to mark off. I think He leaves how we are to live a bit open-ended so we can wrestle with the question, "Lord, what are You asking me to do?"

I've come to believe asceticism is misguided for several reasons. Scripture does not teach that poverty equals godliness. Both the poor and the wealthy need a Savior. In my experience running benevolence ministries at churches, I've run into greedy, selfish, and sinful poor people. That may be politically incorrect to say, but they do exist. Greed and selfishness are conditions of the heart. They're issues we all deal with regardless of our income level.

Asceticism doesn't create godliness. We all have a need for Jesus no matter how much money we make.

Asceticism can also be a form of pride. If you are "showing off" your lack of material possessions to be praised by men, this is self-righteous pride.

A group of Buddhists lives near us at a temple set back off the main road. I've seen them walking barefoot in the cold. But I have also seen them waiting at the bus stop on their cell phones, and I ran across them in the Apple store with their iPads and iPhones. I'm not judging them in any way. I just thought it was funny to see the contrast.

Jesus said:

> Be sure that you not do your charitable deeds before men to be seen by them. Otherwise you have no reward from your Father who is in heaven. Therefore, when you do your charitable deeds, do not sound a trumpet before you as the hypocrites do in the synagogues and in the streets, that they may be honored by men. Truly I say to you, they have their reward.
>
> —MATTHEW 6:1–2, MEV

These verses are telling us that if we give something away, we are not to do it in a way that will draw attention or bring notice. Otherwise, that will be the extent of our reward.

When I was young in ministry, I thought it right as a stewardship pastor to drive really cheap junk cars. Even if it was in terrible shape, if it started, I drove it. My goal was to drive stuff that didn't cost me more than three hundred dollars. My wife hated it. I think I embarrassed her. The cars always leaked something on the driveway. They even occasionally caught on fire! Once I had an Oldsmobile Cutlass with a tear in the vinyl roof. Air would catch in it as I drove. Not only did it look ridiculous, the tear cut my gas mileage to single digits. I lived this way because I thought it made me look more spiritual or godly. It was just another form of pride. I have since repented and bought a nicer, more fuel-efficient car.

Jesus was not an ascetic, but I do believe He was very strategic. He experienced being poor and having poor friends. Yet He was also criticized for His party friends—people who had money and who liked to celebrate.

In Matthew 11:19, Jesus described some of the criticism He received, saying, "The Son of Man came eating and drinking, and they say, 'Here is a glutton and a drunkard, a friend of tax collectors and sinners.' But wisdom is proved by her deeds" (NIV).

Jesus had wealthy friends such as Joseph of Arimathea; Mary, Martha, and Lazarus; Nicodemus; and Zacchaeus. Luke was a physician, Matthew a tax collector, and many of the disciples were successful businessmen, owning boats and homes and having servants.

Jesus was comfortable with the upper-crust folks of His day. He never rebuked people for having stuff. He only rebuked them for not being generous *with* their stuff.

On the other side of the coin is *materialism*, and it is just as dangerous as asceticism, only from the other extreme. The theory behind materialism is that all that exists is matter or energy; everything in life is composed of material and material interactions. The idea is that only the things we can see and feel are genuinely real.

Our culture is very materialistic, and this materialistic worldview has snuck into the church and created problems among believers. Actually materialism runs rampant in the church, and I believe it's why the body of Christ is not more generous as a whole. I believe Christians give only 3 percent of our incomes because we've slipped into these materialistic pitfalls.

Pastor Robert Morris made the observation that people are comfortable saying God owns everything, but when we mention tithing 10 percent, they get upset. Moving from theory to application touches a nerve. All of a sudden, God may not own everything. The thinking seems to be, "You want some of it, Lord? No way—it's *mine!*"

Materialism is greed, and it's rooted in the spirit of mammon. This spirit can drive both materialism and asceticism because it is driven by pride.

## THE SPIRIT OF MAMMON

*Mammon* is an Aramaic word meaning riches. Some believe it comes from the Syrian god of riches and has roots in Babylonian history. One source says the word means "sown in confusion." (As you may recall, Babylon comes from the Tower of Babel.)[5]

When it comes to how we steward money, we are always influenced by one of two spirits: God or mammon. Mammon is a prideful, arrogant spirit that says, "We don't need God." It is the spirit at work when we don't submit our finances to God but use it to replace God.

When we submit our finances to God and don't try to use it to replace Him but to serve Him, our money is blessed. That's why it grows and multiplies and is not devoured by the enemy (Mal. 3:11).

One of the ways mammon manifests itself is through greed. Greed is "the inordinate desire to possess wealth, goods, or objects of abstract value with the intention of keeping it for oneself, far beyond the dictates of basic survival and comfort."[6] Greed is the unholy fruit of the spirit of mammon.

Jesus gives some perspective on how we should view money in a group of scriptures that we all know but may have never put together. In the passage, Jesus is talking about leveraging resources today for kingdom opportunities, which He discusses after sharing the story of the shrewd manager in chapter 16 of Luke's Gospel. Let's pick up the story at verse 9.

> "I tell you, use worldly wealth to gain friends for yourselves, so that when it is gone, you will be welcomed into eternal dwellings. Whoever can be trusted with very little can also be trusted with much, and whoever is dishonest with very little will also be dishonest with much. So if you have not been trustworthy in handling worldly wealth, who will trust you with true riches? And if you have not been trustworthy with someone else's property, who will give you property of your own? No one can serve two masters. Either you will hate the one and love the other, or you will be devoted to the one and despise the other. You cannot serve both God and money."
>
> The Pharisees, who loved money, heard all this and were sneering at Jesus. He said to them, "You are the ones who justify yourselves in the eyes of others, but God knows your hearts. What people value highly is detestable in God's sight."
>
> —LUKE 16:9–15, NIV

Jesus is showing us that how we handle money reveals what's in our hearts. How much we save and how much we keep is all a test of the heart. If we can't give away what God has given us, no matter what the value, we fail the test.

Don't think God would ask you to give up something He gave you? Take a look at the following passage:

> Then Jesus, looking at him, loved him, and said to him, "One thing you lack: Go your way, sell whatever you

> have and give to the poor, and you will have treasure
> in heaven; and come, take up the cross, and follow Me."
> But he was sad at this word, and went away sorrowful,
> for he had great possessions.
> —Mark 10:21–22

The rich young ruler failed the heart test. He may have passed it later on, but if he did, it wasn't recorded in Scripture. Here's another example, this time from the Old Testament:

> Then God said, "Take your son, your only son, whom
> you love—Isaac—and go to the region of Moriah.
> Sacrifice him there as a burnt offering on a mountain I
> will show you."
> —Genesis 22:2, niv

And what did Abraham do? Early the next morning, he got up and loaded his donkey (Gen. 22:3). This is interesting to me because the Bible doesn't tell us that Abraham pushed back in any way. Remember the story of Sodom and Gomorrah? Abraham pushed back five times as he bargained with God over how many righteous men it would take to save the cities. So why didn't He do the same thing when God asked him to sacrifice Isaac?

I believe it was because over the years, Abraham's heart softened, and his faith grew stronger. He had experienced so much of God's blessing that he may have thought, "OK. It sounds like a crazy idea, but I'll do it." He knew God was faithful and would fulfill His promise to him, even if that meant He would raise Isaac from the dead. Abraham didn't have to know why God wanted him to sacrifice Isaac or how He would fulfill His promise. He simply obeyed.

I wonder how many people who upon hearing Abraham's story attempted to do something radical *without* having heard from God. As you can imagine, the results would be tragic.

Luke 12:16–21 has one more example.

> Then He spoke a parable to them, saying: "The ground of a certain rich man yielded plentifully. And he thought within himself, saying, 'What shall I do, since I have no room to store my crops?' So he said, 'I will do this: I will pull down my barns and build greater, and there I will store all my crops and my goods. And I will say to my soul, "Soul, you have many goods laid up for many years; take your ease; eat, drink, and be merry." But God said to him, 'Fool! This night your soul will be required of you; then whose will those things be which you have provided?' "So is he who lays up treasure for himself, and is not rich toward God."

I've heard many teachers say the fool was chastised for saving up, but I don't think that's the point Jesus was trying to make. The fool wasn't chastised for saving. He was chastised for not also being rich toward God. The man was blessed to be a blessing, and he was hoarding his wealth.

Perhaps if he had been rich toward God, the Lord would have blessed him with more. Maybe God would have given him bigger barns strategically because he'd need the resources for something else God wanted him to do. God doesn't have a problem with us saving money and having possessions. The problem arises when we refuse to release what God has given us because our heart is too attached to it.

Is saving money evidence of a lack of faith? Quite the opposite. I think saving money shows evidence of faith in the Word of God. Saving is biblical and is described as the action of a wise person. To not save is described as foolishness. To not save is to presume on the future.

Saving money creates options for the future. How much to save depends on your personal financial margin, position on the Route 7 road map, and calling. But ultimately it is a question to process with God as the owner of your resources.

Consider the following scriptures on saving as we prepare to move forward on Route 7.

> On the first day of every week each one of you is to put aside and save, as he may prosper, so that no collections be made when I come.
> —1 Corinthians 16:2, nas

> Go to the ant, you sluggard! Consider her ways and be wise. Which, having no guide, overseer, or ruler, provides her bread in the summer, and gathers her food in the harvest.
> —Proverbs 6:6–8, mev

> The wise man saves for the future but the foolish man spends whatever he gets.
> —Proverbs 21:20, tlb

> A prudent man sees evil and hides himself, the naive proceed and pay the penalty.
> —Proverbs 27:12, nas

> Four things are small on the earth, but they are exceedingly wise: The ants are not a strong people, but they prepare their food in the summer.
> —Proverbs 30:24–25, nas

> Divide your portion to seven, or even to eight, for you do not know what misfortune may occur on earth.
> —Ecclesiastes 11:2, nas

Several years ago, I had a neighbor who worked for Enron. I always like to ask people what they do for a living because I know they'll ask me the same question. That opens the door for me to talk about church and biblical stewardship, which is something I know they always want to hear about. So after my neighbor told me what he did and I told him I was a stewardship pastor, he asked, kind of sarcastically, if the Bible said anything about investing. I quoted Ecclesiastes 11:2, "Divide your portion to seven, or even to eight, for you do not know what misfortune may occur on earth" (NAS). He thought that was interesting and cool, but he had all his money in Enron stock because they offered a good match on his investment.

"You know that violates biblical principles," I said, noting again that Ecclesiastes tells us not to put all our eggs in one basket but to divide our portion "to seven, or even to eight."

He said, "Yeah, but it's a big company with a good track record." Well, a short time later the whole company fell apart, and he lost the majority of his portfolio. I agree with the writer of Proverbs:

> Give me neither poverty nor riches, but give me only my daily bread, otherwise, I may have too much and disown you and say, "Who is the LORD?" Or I may become poor and steal, and so dishonor the name of my God.
> —PROVERBS 30:8–9, NIV

So, to recap what we've been discussing in this chapter:

- Not saving violates God's Word.

- Poverty *does not* make us more godly.

- Materialism is a spiritual cancer and a mask for a greedy heart.

Follow God in whatever He asks you to do because we are *His* stewards. Sometimes He'll have you save aggressively, perhaps in preparation for something you don't even know is coming, and at other times He may not have you be as aggressive about saving. You must seek His will for yourself and your family through prayer and wise counsel.

I believe your savings is a key to living the blessed life. Remember the quandary I was in when I started researching this chapter? How do we balance saving, giving, and living? Well, I believe our savings is the vehicle through which God empowers us to be generous. When God calls us to give over and above our tithes, that gift comes from our savings. We build up what I call our savings storehouse (more on that in the Route 7 Action Plan at the end of this chapter), and that allows us to have the resources to respond to God's call to give.

We don't need to choose between saving, giving, and living. We tithe, we save, and we live as the Lord leads. We obey God when He leads us to give in excess of our tithe, and we trust Him to take care of the future. In the Route 7 Action Plan, we will look closely at what it means to have a savings storehouse and how to find extra money to save.

## Route 7 Road Map Step 4

1. Create a strategic giving plan.

2. Build a strategic savings storehouse with a short-term savings goal (car replacement, home upgrades, college fund), mid-term savings goal (one-year living expenses), and long-term savings goal (i.e., replacing income through cash-flowing investments).

## YOUR ROUTE 7 ACTION PLAN

A storehouse is a cool concept. Think of it as a barn with multiple sections for storing goods. For our purposes, those goods will be money.

Each section of your savings storehouse is designated for a specific purpose. One could be for college savings, another for an emergency fund of six to twelve months of living expenses, still another for the car payment we're making to ourselves. Missy and I set money aside in accounts designated for our specific savings goal. This way, we're not as likely to give in to the temptation to use that money for something else. It also helps us track our savings and giving goals.

God's Word has a lot to say about storehouses. We read in Genesis 41:56, "When the famine had spread over the whole country, Joseph opened all the *storehouses* and sold grain to the Egyptians, for the famine was severe throughout Egypt" (Gen. 41:56, emphasis added).

God told Joseph to build storehouses all over Egypt to house grain in the time of plenty so there would be food during the coming time of famine.

Deuteronomy 28:12 tells us even God has storehouses: "The LORD will open the heavens, the *storehouse* of his bounty, to send rain on your land in season and to bless all the work of your hands. You will lend to many nations but will borrow from none" (NIV, emphasis added).

A little further in that chapter is a verse I claim for myself, and that I urge you to claim also:

> "The LORD will guarantee a blessing on everything you
> do and will fill your *storehouses* [notice there's more
> than one] with grain. The LORD your God will bless you
> in the land he is giving you."
> —DEUTERONOMY 28:8, NLT, EMPHASIS ADDED

People have asked me how to create a margin, or a financial surplus, to build up their savings. Here are ten tips I often share when asked that question.

# Ten Tips for Saving

1.  Pay God first then save. I've noticed in my own experience and in counseling that when we pay God last, there's not much left for Him. So we pay Him first and pay ourselves second.

2.  Use auto draft to direct deposit your savings. When we do this, we don't see the money so we're not tempted to touch it. Instead, the money goes directly into whatever account we've designated for whatever purpose. We can then make adjustments as our income increases and achieve our financial goals.

3.  Be consistent. It's amazing how much we save when we are consistent about it.

4.  Save for specific purchases rather than putting your savings in one big pile. You can do this by dividing your savings accounts into different categories or by setting up separate accounts.

5.  Set up different savings accounts, even in different banks. This really helps us leave the money alone. Making it hard to get to the money gives us time to think over our options if we are tempted to spend it on something other than what we've designated it for.

6.  Save all your raises and "flatline" your lifestyle. When you determine to live on a certain amount, any raises or extra income you get can go directly into savings. Missy and I are living on the income we earned four years ago. The difference from all my raises goes into savings.

7. Pray about your savings. Seek His wisdom and guidance as to how much you should save. Some people say you should save 10 percent, but I don't believe one size fits all when it comes to savings. Save what the Lord impresses on your heart to put aside for the season you are in.

8. Give from your savings, as the Lord leads.

9. Add any decrease in your monthly expenses to your savings. For example, after shopping around, I was able to cut our car insurance premium in half. All that extra money went into savings.

10. Save as you pay off debt. Devote a set amount to savings and another amount to eliminating debt. As you pay off a debt, you can add that extra money to savings to avoid going back into debt when something breaks. This requires steady plodding, but it is so worth it. One thousand dollars isn't much of an emergency fund these days. When was the last time you went through a year with only a thousand dollars' worth of emergencies? I strongly believe in automatic, regular savings to keep out of additional debt and to build up your storehouse so you'll have money to give.

You may be wondering why I focused on saving before debt. It's simple—because understanding the importance of saving is critical to getting and staying out of debt. Debt undermines our ability to give freely, which is our ultimate aim, so in the next chapter we will tackle the issue of debt head-on.

# Chapter 7

# A BIBLICAL VIEW OF DEBT

L ET ME BE up front with you: I hate debt! I see debt as a form of bondage that keeps us tied to the lender and interferes with our ability to accomplish all God desires for us. The stress of debt leads to fear, poor communication, poor decision-making, and damaged relationships—sometimes beyond repair.

If you are struggling with debt, I have no desire to condemn you. I want to help you get free. Read on with me as I unpack the biblical view of debt and give some options to help you develop a plan to get out.

## WHAT IS DEBT?

As always in this book, I want to first establish our scriptural foundation. So let's look at five words associated with debt to better understand what the Bible is telling us about this topic.

### Debt

A *debt* is something owed. Anyone who has borrowed money or goods from someone else owes a debt and is under obligation to return the goods or repay the money, usually with interest.

The Israelites knew a thing or two about the yoke of debt. In Nehemiah's day, things were a mess in Israel, and the people were crying out because of the debt they were forced to bear. "We are mortgaging our fields, our vineyards and our houses that we might get grain because of the famine," they cried. "We have borrowed money for the king's tax on our field and our vineyards." (See Nehemiah 5:3–4.)

They were borrowing money to pay their taxes and they were borrowing grain to keep from starving. Their sons and daughters were being forced into slavery to pay off debt. And they felt helpless to do anything about it because their fields and vineyards belonged to others.

This was in no way God's intention—and it still isn't.

There are many modern parallels. In many parts of our world, children are sold into sex trafficking to pay off family debts. The economic crises in Cyprus, Greece, Spain, and Portugal look strangely similar to the Israelites' situation in Nehemiah's day. While those nations are not in the position of selling off family members to cover debts, they are in the process of making deep, painful cuts to survive crushing financial obligations. What gives me great concern is the speed at which the United States is following in their footsteps with our out-of-control debt.

In Matthew 18:26–33 Jesus tells us of an unmerciful servant. His master forgave him a huge debt, yet the servant turned around and demanded that another servant pay him a niggling little debt or be thrown into prison. Debt can distort our perspective and our sense of justice.

In Ezekiel 18:7–9 a righteous man is described as one who restores the debtor and does not lend money on interest, among other qualities. The Bible tells us such a man will surely live. Being in debt is no way to live, which brings us to the second term.

## Borrow

*Borrowing* is taking and using something that belongs to someone else with the intention of returning it. It also includes borrowing money with the intent of repaying the amount with interest. The Lord doesn't mind borrowing—as long as we're not the ones on the borrowing side. Consider the following verses:

> You will not borrow; and you will rule over many nations but they will not rule over you.
> —DEUTERONOMY 15:6, NAS

> You shall lend to many nations, but you shall not borrow.
> —DEUTERONOMY 28:12, NAS

> The borrower becomes the lender's slave.
> —PROVERBS 22:7, NAS

The Bible makes it clear that it's a blessing to be a lender, but "the borrower becomes the lender's slave." That doesn't sound like blessed living to me.

## Surety

*Surety* is a word we don't hear too much anymore, but the concept is very alive in today's society. I'm in surety when I have become legally responsible for the debt, default, or failure of someone else. We call it *cosigning*, usually for someone's car or personal note. God is very clear about this:

> Do not be among those who give pledges, among those who become guarantors for debts.
> —PROVERBS 22:26, NAS

Earlier in Proverbs, the Lord advises, "If you've already cosigned, get out of it as quickly as possible. If you have been caught by the words of your mouth...deliver yourself. Since you have come into the hand of your neighbor, go, humble yourself, and importune your neighbor." (See Proverbs 6:1–4.)

When cosigning goes bad, it will ruin your credit as well as the person's you cosign for, and it will hurt the relationship in the process. The primary warning sign is this: If the person had good credit, they wouldn't need you to cosign!

## Usury

*Usury* is the lending of money with an interest charged for its use. This often refers to a loan with an exorbitant interest rate. Think of those sub-prime credit cards, payday loans, or unsecured loans that charge high interest rates, frequently over 30 percent. In Proverbs 28:8, the Lord tells us, "One who increases his possessions by usury and extortion gathers it for him who will pity the poor."

## Lending

*Lending* refers to loaning money to others for temporary use usually on the condition that it be repaid with interest. In Deuteronomy 15:8 we are told, "You shall freely open your hand to him and shall generously lend him sufficient for his need in whatever he lacks" (NAS). Psalm 112:5 says, "It is well with a man who is gracious and lends" (NAS). Nehemiah 5:10 goes further: "We have been lending money and grain to the people, but let's stop this charging interest" (NLT).

In the Old Testament, debt was considered a form of slavery. There was a provision in the Law that every fifty years, during the year of Jubilee, they were to be forgiven their debt. However, there is no biblical record that a year of Jubilee was ever actually celebrated.[1]

The Israelites also were not to charge interest to fellow Hebrews, but they could charge the Gentiles interest. One of my Jewish friends told me God created Gentiles so someone could pay interest! To be a lender is a blessing; to be a borrower is a curse, or at least an indication you are in hard times.

In Nehemiah's day, having a mortgage on your property was a sign of desperation. Things have sure changed over the centuries. Nowadays, it's rare to hear of someone actually paying cash for a home. Did you know the word "mortgage" is actually a combination of the words *mort* (death) and *gage* (pledge)! Mortgage literally means "death pledge."[2]

The most direct passage on debt in the New Testament is in Romans.

> Owe no one anything, except to love one another, for he who loves another has fulfilled the law.
> —ROMANS 13:8, MEV

Some argue that this verse doesn't really apply to financial debt. But if you read Romans 13 in context, Paul is clearly talking about submitting to governing authorities and paying taxes.

In Jesus's day, just as today, debt was a hot topic. Many of His parables and teachings touched on the subject of finances and debt. This is because finances and debt deeply affected people's lives. It wasn't unusual for people to be indentured or put in debtors' prison or sold as slaves if they were unable to pay their debt. For many there was no way out of debt.

Jesus used the pervasiveness of debt to teach people the truth about forgiveness of sin. He told them that just as there was no way out of debt there was no way out of sin except through Christ. Just as they couldn't pay their debt, they couldn't pay their way out of sin.

Our Lord also counseled us not to turn away from someone who wants to borrow from us if we can help the person (Matt. 5:42, NLT). And He encourages us to forgive others' debts as others, including God, forgive us. In other words, be as generous as He has been to us.

To summarize, the Bible clearly discourages borrowing, but it is not forbidden or considered sin. (It would make a stewardship pastor's job easier if it were, but I digress.) Lending is a blessing, but borrowing places us in a master/servant role with a creditor. At a bare minimum, according to Scripture, debt should be used in an ultra-conservative manner.

The first time I borrowed money from my dad, our relationship underwent a fundamental change to this master/servant arrangement, which was very uncomfortable for both of us. It felt awkward to call home and talk about money I used for anything other than paying him back. I wanted to pay him back quickly and get our relationship on its correct footing. And I did.

Under the biblical plan, our goal is to get completely out of debt. This will take time, planning, and careful stewardship of our money. The ideal position is to have no debt and to have a significant enough financial margin to be flexible to follow the Holy Spirit's leading.

I encourage you not to develop your theology about debt from one verse—or even one man's teaching. Take a full view of the Scriptures to form your own view on the subject. As I said in an earlier chapter, I don't want to talk you into agreeing with me. I want you to discover for yourself what the Word of God says so being debt-free becomes a personal conviction.

Early in my position as a pastor, a young man I counseled wanted desperately to go into the mission field. He had a heart for missions and a zeal for the Lord. He also had over $100,000 in student loans. The mission board turned him down because there was no way he could go into the mission field and afford to repay his debt. He was heartbroken—he couldn't pursue that ministry opportunity because of debt.

There is a definite connection between debt and your calling. Missy and I knew the Lord had called us to get completely out of debt before I went into full-time ministry. Using the debt snowball strategy, we paid off $88,000 of debt, which was everything we owed except the house. The month I made the last payment on the debt is when I got the call to interview for my first full-time ministry position.

The new position came with a significant pay cut. I wouldn't have been able to take the position if we were still in debt. We couldn't have afforded it. But because we were debt-free, we were able to rearrange our lifestyle and answer the call to full-time ministry.

That does not mean God cannot use a person in ministry if he is in debt. But I believe He wants us to prepare financially to fulfill the call He has put on our lives.

## ONE NATION IN DEBT

Unfortunately most Americans are falling deep into debt. Here are some numbers that boggled my mind when I first read them.

In 2010 the total consumer debt stood at $2.4 *trillion*! That's an average debt of $7,800 for every man, woman, and child. One-third of that is revolving debt such as credit cards. This means it just cycles and recycles every month. Actually, it acts more like a spiral, always going up. The other two-thirds is debt such as car loans, student loans, and mortgages.[3]

It is amazing to me that in 2005 some $33.2 billion worth of fast food was charged, and in 2006 it jumped to $51 billion—an increase of nearly 54 percent. We as Americans are rapidly increasing our debt to buy food. And it's not even for basic groceries. It's for Big Macs and Whoppers.[4]

Credit cards seem to be taking over the world. Statistics show the average consumer has four credit cards. Ten percent have more than ten cards. The average household carries an average of $6,500 in credit card debt from month to month.[5]

When I teach about debt in churches, we end the class with a ceremony during which we cut up our credit cards. One couple had over sixty credit cards! I talked with them later, and the husband told me he saw himself as a success because all those cards showed him that someone saw him as valuable and worthy. Until that night, his goal had been to get as many credit cards as possible. Now his worth is based on his relationships with God and his family, not how much plastic he carries.

Another counselee came to me eaten up with stress about her finances. She had fallen into the pattern of using one credit card to pay off another and had accumulated $110,000 of credit card debt with no way to pay it off. She couldn't keep floating the debt because all her cards were maxed out. And now the creditors were calling. She handled all the finances in the home, and her husband didn't know anything about what was going on, and she was scared to tell him. I called the couple into my office and together she and I explained the situation. He freaked out and was really upset. Can you blame him?

Then I told him it was his fault. He was not really happy to hear that either, but he listened. By leaving all the finances in his wife's hands, he had abdicated his leadership mantle in the family. He hadn't been involved in managing his household finances and put his wife under such stress she couldn't even talk to him about it. Even if they agreed that she would handle the day-to-day money management, he should have been knowledgeable of their financial position.

He was brokenhearted after we spoke, and they prayed and repented. They took financial classes and participated in counseling and other programs we offered through the church. Eventually they did have to file bankruptcy but rebuilt their lives and finances on Christian principles. The last time I saw them, they were walking through church holding hands whereas before she would walk six feet behind him because she has such low self-esteem.

Our nation as a whole doesn't appear to be in much better shape than its citizens. At the time of this writing, the total

US government debt is $18 trillion! It took our country more than two hundred years to reach $1 trillion in debt. But in just over thirty years, we added another $17 trillion. And it's not just one party doing it. President Reagan added $1.8 trillion of debt in his eight years.[6] President George W. Bush added $4.9 trillion over eight years. President Obama added $7.5 trillion as of April 2015.[7] This irresponsibility cannot continue. I am not making a political statement; simple mathematics say it cannot continue. The country needs to wake up and elect responsible leaders on both sides of the aisle who will govern as good stewards.[8]

## My Philosophy on Debt

As you can no doubt tell, the whole idea of getting out of debt is very real and personal for me. My goal is to be debt-free—mortgage and all, as the Lord blesses. Missy and I are striving to live out a plan where we save one-third of our money, give away one-third, and live on one-third. This is requiring some serious discipline and lifestyle adjustments, but we believe it is achievable.

We don't use unsecured loans or credit cards as part of our personal budget. I'm not saying using credit cards is a sin (though it may be for some people who abuse them). Each of us has to wrestle with this issue for ourselves, but I'm a firm advocate of not using credit cards. They open the door to all kinds of problems and temptations we don't need. My wife and I also have decided to never cosign a loan for anyone else. To do so violates biblical teaching.

By saving aggressively, we'll be able to guard and increase our margin so we'll be in a position to respond to God's leading as soon as He speaks.

Any major financial decisions we make, such as buying cars or homes and paying for college for our kids, will be done with a multitude of counselors. Obviously Missy and I have to come into agreement about the decision. But we will also talk with other people we trust regarding certain financial issues.

We talk with spiritual counselors and leaders to make sure we're understanding what the Lord is saying and not just reacting to last night's pizza. We have financial planners who help us with our long-range goals. We work with our certified public accountant (CPA) to stay on top of our financial situation and to make sure we're doing the right things with the money God gives us.

I think it's pretty clear I'm a bit of a car freak, so before I plunge into buying a car I talk with a car expert who knows me well and knows my tendencies to buy and sell cars. We have a strong relationship, so he won't hesitate to tell me if I'm doing something stupid. In the same way, we have a home expert who loves us enough to speak straight about our thinking regarding buying a new home or remodeling what we have. As Proverbs 11:14 says, "Where there is no counsel, the people fall; but in the multitude of counselors there is safety" (MEV).

If I'm embarrassed to tell someone what I'm doing financially, then I probably shouldn't be doing it. Missy and I have financial accountability from multiple angles. Each relationship has taken time to develop, but we were intentional about building these accountability partnerships. First we prayed for a group of godly counselors. Then I wrote a list of the financial fields for which I wanted to develop accountability relationships to seek wisdom at decision crossroads.

In the end God blessed Missy and me to build relationships with:

### Prayer partners

We asked a couple of families if they would pray for us. I send them ministry updates and ask for prayer feedback. They cover any and everything in our life with prayer. We stay in close relationship, getting together for dinner each month and having randomly timed phone calls throughout the month.

## A financial advisor

We work with a financial planner who is close to our age but has a lot of industry experience. We set goals together, and he holds us accountable to them. I recommend finding a financial planner through Kingdom Advisors (www.kingdom advisors.org). These individuals are trained and committed to giving advice from a biblical perspective to help people make wise financial decisions and be faithful stewards.

## A certified public accountant

I can prepare our taxes, but if I did, I would miss out on the wisdom of our CPA. He not only helps us at tax time, but he is a key counselor to help us set and meet our financial goals.

## A car counselor

Every time I get the car bug or need to make a car decision, I process the decision with my car guru friend who happens to be in the car business. Even if I do not buy a car through him, I still process my thoughts with him. When I have made car decisions without his input, it has cost me money!

## A home counselor

I don't make many home decisions, but I have found a friend who is really sharp about real estate. He can help me assess the area, timing, interest rates, and whether or not to upgrade items. It is his area of expertise, and he always gives me things to think about that I had not previously considered. He also is a good enough friend to tell me I am about to make a bad decision.

Make your own list of financial counselors and pray for God to put the wise individuals in your path. You may have different needs than we do, and your lists will change as your life seasons change. For instance, I don't need a retirement expert to help me preserve the retirement nest egg—yet. One day I will. And because I no longer own a business, my need for business counsel is limited. But that may be the primary area for which you need a good counselor. Seek the Lord for the right counsel for your situation.

## COMMON FORMS OF DEBT

Debt comes in many forms, and every time we sign up for a debt, we're signing up to be a slave to whoever holds the note, whether it's a bank, a credit union, a friend, or a family member. We are entering into an unequal relationship because that institution or person now holds power over our money and us. If you do not believe me, just miss a few payments, and you will feel the puppet master pull the strings.

I want to explain several common forms of debt to help you see how they can keep you in financial bondage.

### Payday loans

These are short-term, unsecured loans that charge super high interest. While they seem inexpensive at the start, the annual interest rate can be over 300 percent. Below are examples of annual percentage rates (APR) popular Texas lenders charge for a two-week loan period.[9]

| LENDER | AMOUNT BORROWED | APR | FINANCE CHARGES |
|---|---|---|---|
| PAY DAY ONE | $100<br>$200<br>$500<br>$1000 | 598.51%<br>596.64%<br>596.62%<br>596.62% | $22.88<br>$45.77<br>$114.42<br>$225.24 |
| CASH NET USA | $100<br>$200<br>$500<br>$1000 | 664.29%<br>664.29%<br>664.29%<br>664.29% | $25.48<br>$50.96<br>$127.60<br>$254.79 |
| NCP FINANCE LIMITED PARTNERSHIP | $100<br>$200<br>$500<br>$1000 | 641.59%<br>641.59%<br>641.59%<br>641.59% | $25.38<br>$50.75<br>$126.91<br>$253.83 |
| MIDWEST R&S CORPORATION | $100<br>$200<br>$500<br>$1000 | 583.45%<br>583.45%<br>583.45%<br>583.45% | $22.38<br>$44.74<br>$111.91<br>$223.43 |

Understandably there is a very high default rate with these loans, and it is extremely hard to get out of this debt. You either have to get a large cash influx or squeeze your monthly budget to get out of the loan. You may have to get a second job just to gain enough momentum to pay off the loan. Either way, these are tough to pay off. It's better not to enter them from the start.

**Credit cards**

With their ninety-day, no-interest teasers or balance transfer incentives, credit cards lead to impulse buying. Studies have shown that people who use plastic frequently purchase more than those who used cash.[10] It just feels easier to throw an extra burger or dessert in the bag when it seems like we're not forking over real money. But it will get real when the bill arrives!

Recently Missy and I took a trip to New Mexico. We took

$250 in cash for meals and entertainment. We came home with sixty dollars because we managed cash differently than we would have managed a credit card. Cash is harder to spend. We could see it leave the wallet and not come back. Because we had cash, we made wiser decisions and still had great time.

At one time, 84 percent of college students had credit cards, according to a Sallie Mae study, even though most of them had not established any credit history.[11] They had little income, so they rapidly maxed their cards out and ran up fees that kept them tied to the credit card company for years. The Credit Card Act banned credit card approvals for anyone under twenty-one years old unless they have an adult cosigner or can prove they have sufficient income to pay the bills. Though the situation has improved, the passage of that bill hasn't prevented students from getting into credit card debt. The average balance among college students in 2013 was $499.[12]

Credit card debt is a touchy subject. I read a study recently that said credit card debt is at the top of the list of things people don't want to talk about (right up there with details of your love life). This is one reason credit card debt is such a burden. People carry the emotional and spiritual weight of that debt privately.

And despite recent efforts to control credit card companies, the collection practices of these businesses are awful. If you run late with a payment, you could be subjected to repeated and harassing phone calls, threatening letters, and various types of coercion to get as much money out of you as possible. I recently met with sisters whose mother was dying. The mom was in the last days of her life, and her daughters were dealing with this intensely emotional and personal crisis. Yet a credit card company was calling repeatedly and getting ugly, trying to manipulate the children into giving them some of Mom's money before she went to heaven. It is unbelievable to me how aggressive these companies can be when collecting overdue payments.

**Home loans**

These are also known as mortgages. You may remember the word mortgage comes from the Latin terms *mort* (death) and *gage* (pledge), which leaves us with "death pledge." Think about that. You're making a death pledge with your finances.

Most of us don't have $100,000 to pay cash for a house, so it's likely you will need to take out a mortgage to buy your home. That said, I recommend people take out fifteen-year mortgages, or shorter ones if possible. The longer your mortgage, the more interest you pay and the more likely you are to give the holder much more money than the house costs.

At the end of the chapter in our Route 7 Action Plan, we will talk about creating a strategy to get out of debt. Many people think they're home free after they've paid off their credit cards and student loans. But after those debts are paid and you've built up your savings to one year of living expenses, I encourage people to then focus on paying off their mortgage early.

It is important to build up your savings storehouse before attacking the mortgage. I've worked with several families who actually over-focused on paying off the mortgage. When they lost their jobs, they didn't have enough in their savings or emergency fund to float them along until they got a new job. Many went into foreclosure or had to short-sale their house as a result.

**Home equity loans and lines of credit**

These loans tap into the equity in your house—the difference between what you owe on your house and what you can sell it for—to provide a source of cash. It's actually credit, and it's based on the assumption your house will continue to increase in value. Well, the last few years have shown that's not a dependable premise. Banks pushed these loans, and people treated their houses like never-ending piggy banks. One bank told me I would never have to worry about balancing my checkbook because I could just tap into my line of credit if I came up short. Unfortunately even if you're up to date on your first mortgage, lenders can still take you into foreclosure if you fall behind on these lines of credit.

**Business debt**

When I teach these stewardship principles to groups that include business leaders, someone will inevitably say you can't run a business without business debt. I disagree. I *know* you can run a business without debt because I did it with my construction business in Florida. You can plan your business finances the same way you plan your family's finances—save up for the startup costs and spend only what comes in. It takes a lot of work and diligence, but it can be done—especially with the business tools available today. Several large companies operate debt-free, including T. Rowe Price, Bed, Bath & Beyond, and MasterCard (which is kind of ironic considering their business model is based on your debt).[13]

A few years back, Walgreens and Eckerd drug stores were in heavy competition. They were building on opposite corners of the same block and competing ferociously for business. There was one major difference between them—Walgreens was debt-free. They had the margin to sustain the battle. Eckerd was loaded with debt and didn't have the ability to keep up with the competition. It eventually collapsed, and half of it was sold to CVS.[14]

The moral of the story is clear. Don't think business debt is inevitable. If you are diligent to operate debt-free, it is possible.

**Ministry debt**

I offer the same encouragement to churches. Ministry debt can become as financially, emotionally, and spiritually burdensome as business debt. And it can lead to strife and division within a congregation. Many churches seem to think, "If we build it, they will come." This is not always true, especially when there is no real need to build. It's a misperception that new buildings will draw new people. My counsel to churches is to build only when there are actual growth problems. When a ministry has run out of room, they should first get creative in how they use their space, then they should build.

When the decision to build has been made, the church must be very conservative with construction and develop a plan from the beginning to get out of debt. Borrowing should be limited to 1 percent of the church's annual revenue. Gateway Church is working toward its goal of being completely debt-free. Even though we have borrowed to manage growth, we have secured a short-term loan (ten years vs. the industry average of twenty to twenty-five years), and our debt service amount is under 10 percent of our yearly budget. That's pretty conservative.

### Student loans

I am not a fan of student loans. Recent history shows how expensive and burdensome they are. Some students are graduating with more than $100,000 in student loan debt and entering a job market with few prospects to earn enough to pay it off. Student loans are very hard to pay off—and the lenders can garnish up to 15 percent of your wages if you lag in paying them.[15]

If you absolutely must go to college to pursue your career goals, find a way to work through college and not accrue debt. Consider working for a year or two to save money. Believe me, the life experience of working and putting your own skin in the game to pursue your dream is invaluable. And you won't have to pay thousands and thousands of dollars in interest.

If you have student loans, live like you did when you were

in school—as frugally as possible—and pay off the debt using a debt snowball, which I will explain in the Route 7 Road Map at the end of this chapter.

When I graduated from high school, I had some partial scholarship opportunities, but they weren't enough to cover the full cost of college. Even at that age, I did not feel comfortable taking on the debt of a student loan. So I didn't take on any loans and only took one class. Instead of continuing in college, I started a business and made a good living. Life kind of derailed the college dream, but I always knew that someday I'd have the chance to go back. In the meantime, God trained me to do what I'm doing now. About two years ago my faithfulness was rewarded when the elders of Gateway offered to bless me if I wanted to go back to college. So God has made a way for me to get my education, in part because of my faithfulness and obedience to His call.

**Family loans**

These should be avoided at all costs—and I do mean *all*. Family loans usually turn into a disaster and can severely strain, if not destroy, relationships. No amount of money is worth years of estrangement and bitterness. Scripture says the borrower is the slave to the lender, and do you really want Grandma to be the master of *your* universe?

**Back taxes**

Another harsh master is the IRS. If they say you owe them money, you are guilty until proven innocent, and you're probably in for a long, hard battle. The government can garnish wages and take property to pay the debt. So keep careful records and pay your taxes accurately.

The Bible tells us we have a responsibility to pay our debts. Psalm 37:21 says, "The wicked borrows and does not repay, but the righteous is gracious and gives" (MEV).

For many, bankruptcy seems to provide a way out of financial turmoil, but it is no longer the panacea it once was. The laws have been updated, and it is very difficult to successfully file for personal bankruptcy (commonly referred to as Chapter 7). There is now a means test you must meet.[16] If you make over a certain preset amount, you will be given a repayment plan. And you will still be responsible for spousal and child support, some taxes, and student loans. It no longer rids you of all debt.

A Chapter 13 bankruptcy is actually a debt reorganization process. The debt is not abolished. It is restructured to satisfy your creditors. A Chapter 11 bankruptcy is a reorganization of business debt.

Our bankruptcy laws have their origin in the biblical concepts of the sabbatical year and the Year of Jubilee. But filing bankruptcy isn't the same as a Jubilee year. Many who have filed bankruptcy have told me it is almost as tough as getting divorced.

There are many good reasons to avoid debt, but what happens if that ship has sailed and you're already saddled with student loans, high credit card balances, and other types of debt? Keep reading, because in our Route 7 Action Plan we will discuss how to end the debt cycle for good.

## Route 7 Road Map Step 5

1.  Continue your strategic giving plan.
2.  Evaluate your calling. (Is the Lord calling you to go back to college, start a business, or change careers?)
3.  Invest (build assets that create cash flow).
4.  Begin paying extra toward your mortgage.

## YOUR ROUTE 7 ACTION PLAN

Debt cannot always be avoided, especially when it comes to buying a house. Before you make any decisions about taking on debt, there are four questions you need to ask yourself. These are four areas to discuss with your spouse and your accountability partners. If you're single, I urge you to develop a relationship with someone you feel very comfortable with in discussing your finances. The decision to take on debt is not one you should make alone.

### 1. The Tomorrow Test

James 4:13–16 says, "Look here, you who say, 'Today or tomorrow we are going to a certain town and will stay there a year. We will do business there and make a profit.' How do you know what your life will be like tomorrow? Your life is like the morning fog—it's here a little while, then it's gone. What you ought to say is, 'If the Lord wants us to, we will live and do this or that.' Otherwise you are boasting about your own plans, and all such boasting is evil" (NLT). The Tomorrow Test asks:

- If my income is cut next year, can I still pay this loan off on schedule?

- If I lost my job and had to take another job making a lot less, could I still afford this loan?

- Am I making this decision based on a hope of future income, no matter how secure or insecure it might be?

Never take a loan expecting any kind of financial increase. If you do, you will fail the Tomorrow Test.

## 2. The Security Test
For this test ask yourself:

- If I have to sell the asset, will I make enough to cover what I owe on it?

- Do I have equity in the asset?

In other words, the loan must be much less than the value of whatever item is purchased.

## 3. The Freedom Test
To take this test, ask yourself:

- Does this loan restrict my freedom or limit me in any way? Does it hinder my financial, emotional, or spiritual freedom?

- Does this loan limit my ability to give, change jobs, or move in any way God directs? Many times God is trying to get us to slow down so He can show an option that doesn't involve going into debt. We need to be patient and wait to hear what He has to say to us.

- Does this debt build or hurt my testimony? Does it show God shining forth in my life?

## 4. The Dependence Test
Ask yourself:

- By taking this debt, am I forcing myself into a position of being dependent on others?

- Who am I depending on, man or God?

- Am I going around God's already provided provision?

- Am I willing to wait on Him or must I have the item now?

I've counseled people who took the time to take these four simple tests. Before we take on debt, we need to take a step back and consider our current financial state. Then we have to prayerfully make a plan for how we'll stay out of debt.

## BREAK THE DEBT CYCLE

Even though debt cannot always be avoided, you should always have a strategy for getting out of debt and staying out of debt. Below are six tips for breaking the cycle of debt.

### 1. Give.

Giving changes our hearts. And giving injects the Lord's provision into our lives. Scripture says, "Give, and it will be given to you: Good measure, pressed down, shaken together, and running over will men give unto you. For with the measure you use, it will be measured unto you" (Luke 6:38, MEV). The Lord is faithful to provide for those who are givers.

### 2. Change your spending habits.

Determine to live on less than you earn so you can create a financial margin. Missy and I live on a *written* budget, and we avoid magazines, television shows, and websites that fuel our desires to make purchases. I easily get the car bug and want to start shopping for another vehicle. When this happens, I've learned to stay away from auto magazines and websites about cars because I know I will talk myself into buying a car before my finances are ready. For some living on less may mean modifying your lifestyle as we discussed at the end of chapter 4. Use the strategies for reducing expenses found in chapter 4's Route 7 Action Plan. This way you can increase your margin and use that surplus to pay off debt.

## 3. Commit to not creating any new debt.

Cut up the credit cards and determine you're not going into debt for anything else. As we keep making payments above the minimum and use the debt snowball plan I explain in number 5 of this list, eventually we will get out of debt. Then we can use all the money we've been paying out to increase our margin and our giving.

## 4. Communicate honestly and frequently with your spouse and accountability partner.

Get to know your spouse's spending patterns and talk openly about them—nicely. Don't make impulse buys. Commit to calling each other before making a purchase over a certain amount. For Missy and me, that amount is thirty dollars. And don't buy on emotion.

One day I realized that while I love to buy and sell cars, I couldn't stay content with a car for very long. I approached an elder in the church, and we prayed about it. I asked God if there was a reason I struggled with contentment when it came to cars. The elder told me God had shown him it had something to do with a red sports car and an experience I had in high school.

When he said that, a memory came back to me. A friend of mine had a red sports car, and she would let me borrow it during the last period of the day. I had a blast joyriding around town before returning it to her at the end of the school day.

One day we ended up in a very ugly conversation and she said, "At least my parents can afford to send me to this private school." That stung because my parents struggled to pay my tuition, and I also received financial aid from the school. Back then I made a vow to always be self-sufficient and to always drive a very nice car. I was viewing my self-worth by what I drove instead of what God had put in me. Once I confessed my wrong and dealt with the root issue, I became much more content with my cars.

If you struggle in a particular area, ask the Lord to show you if there is a reason you are having a hard time being content. Your debt patterns may just be symptoms of deeper issues that you need to explore with your spouse or pastoral staff.

## 5. Create a debt snowball plan.

List your debts from smallest to largest. Make minimum payments on the larger ones as you attack the smallest debt first. Sell things. Pull money from your budget, and use it to pay off the smallest debt by analyzing every line in the budget to see if there is any way to trim something from the category. A little here and there can add up. When you've paid off the first one, take that payment and add it to the payment on the next highest debt. Keep doing that until all the debt is paid off.

## 6. Save, save, save.

Save as much as you can, whenever you can. Remember, a budget gives every dollar a name and a purpose. Name some of it *savings*.

Getting out of debt takes patience, planning, and diligence. You didn't get into debt overnight, so don't expect to get out of it overnight either. But commit to doing it. Apply the principles we've taught in this chapter and this book, and you will become debt-free. And you will find that you love paying cash for things.

As we've discussed, putting your finances in order is just a means for you to gain the freedom to follow God's calling on your life. But what if you don't know what that calling is? How do you make a plan if you don't know where you're headed? In the next chapter we are going to answer those questions as we look at another very important type of stewardship.

# Chapter 8
# LIFE STEWARDSHIP

S O FAR IN this book we've been talking about financial stewardship, but I want to turn your attention to another kind of stewardship: life stewardship.

Life stewardship is living out God's calling on your life. He didn't place us here to scurry meaninglessly through life like mice in a maze. He has a plan for each of us—a plan for us personally and a plan for us to reveal Him to others to draw them closer to Him.

But what is that plan? There are many people who think, "I'm doing well financially, but I'm not sure I'm fulfilling my calling in life." They find themselves saying, "I don't know why I'm here. I don't know what God wants me to do. Does He even have a specific plan for my life?"

The answer is, "Yes, He does."

"Well, Pastor Gunnar, how do I figure out what it is?"

I'm so glad you asked. After all, if you don't know where you're headed, if you don't know how God wired you, why go to all the trouble of getting out of debt? Why get your finances in order just to reach a box canyon of not knowing why you've done this?

Many times, finding our calling feels like flying in the dark. When I was eighteen years old, I took flying lessons. And it was fun hopping around in little Cessnas—until I had to fly at night over the ocean! That was downright scary. The lighting in the plane is dim, and it's difficult to find the horizon. If the moon is shining, its reflection off the water creates distraction and confusion, which is a dangerous thing to deal with while flying a plane. It messes with your head, and you can't tell which direction is up. One moon is in the sky, the other is in the water, and it's hard to tell which one is real. If you aim for the wrong moon, you could be heading for the water.

The only way to survive is to rely on the gauges in the plane—on the altimeter and the other instruments that tell you exactly where you are. A pilot has to trust them. He must have faith that the gauges work and are accurate.

It's the same in life. Sometimes the direction feels right, but we're headed toward the water. Just as pilots rely on their instruments to fly, in life we have to rely on our instruments—our relationship with God and His Word.

When seeking God's calling on our life, it's far more important to discover who we *are* over what we *do*. What we *do* is the outflow of who we *are*. Who we *are* in life needs to be channeled through our God-given gifts into what we *do*. Another way to look at it is this: once we figure out who we are, our natural God-given gifts are developed into skills we use to serve Him and help others.

In the remainder of this chapter, I want to share several insights I've gained that I believe will help you identify your calling and be a good life steward.

## Know Who You Are in Christ

The first step in discovering God's calling on your life is to know your identity. That means you must first answer this question: Do you know Christ? If you do, your identity is spectacular. If you don't know Him, then you're in trouble. The Scriptures tell us:

Therefore, if anyone is in Christ, he is a new creation. The old has passed away; behold, the new has come.

—2 CORINTHIANS 5:17, ESV

There is therefore now no condemnation for those who are in Christ Jesus.

—ROMANS 8:1, ESV

But you are a chosen race, a royal priesthood, a holy nation, a people for his own possession, that you may proclaim the excellencies of him who called you out of darkness into his marvelous light.

—1 PETER 2:9, ESV

Do not be conformed to this world, but be transformed by the renewal of your mind, that by testing you may discern what is the will of God, what is good and acceptable and perfect.

—ROMANS 12:2, ESV

But to all who did receive him, who believed in his name, he gave the right to become children of God.

—JOHN 1:12, ESV

For our sake he made him to be sin who knew no sin, so that in him we might become the righteousness of God.

—2 CORINTHIANS 5:21, ESV

When we bundle these passages together, we get a glimpse of who we are in Christ. We are new creations with transformed minds; we are a royal priesthood, children of God, and in Christ, the righteousness of God. This identity should cause us to get us out of bed in the morning feeling pretty good about ourselves. Our identity is pretty spectacular, and it's all made possible by knowing Jesus's work on the cross. We're amazingly gifted, called by Christ, and worthy of His sacrifice. We have a Bible full of words of affirmation of who we are in Christ.

## DISCOVER YOUR GIFTS

Ephesians 2:10 tells us, "For we are His workmanship, *created in Christ Jesus for good works*, which God prepared beforehand, so that we should walk in them" (MEV, emphasis added). So if you're wondering what works you were created to do and what your gifts are, you need to become a student of yourself and of God's Word. You need to figure out what makes you tick and how you're wired.

You may have heard the saying, "Love your neighbor as you love yourself" (Luke 10:27; Matt. 22:39; Mark 12:30–31). The problem is many people don't know how to love themselves, so they don't know how to love God or others. God made us "fearfully and wonderfully" (Ps. 139:14, KJV), and He loves who He made. None of us are perfect, and we should always grow to become more like Jesus. But we must also recognize and appreciate our God-given gifts, talents, and abilities, because He wants us to use them for His glory. So how can we discover who we are and identify our gifts? Here are some tips.

### Find your strengths.

Management and leadership guru Peter Drucker once wrote: "Most people think they know what they are good at. They are usually wrong.... And yet, a person can perform only from strength."[1]

Have you ever met someone who thinks he's really good at a sport like basketball or tennis or golf? Then you play with the person and find out he's really awful. This is what Drucker is talking about.

A few years ago, scientists tested freshmen who were entering prestigious colleges. They found basically two groups of students. What separated them was how fast they read. One read 90 words per minute. The other read roughly 270 words per minute. The scientists knew students needed to be able to read quickly if they were going to make it in college, so they put all the students through six weeks of speed-reading classes. The theory was the students in the ninety-word-per-minute group would catch up to the 270 group.

They at first thought their experiment was a success. The 90-word-per-minute group did improve—to nearly 300 words per minute!

Then they retested the 270 group. Their scores soared to over *2,700 words per minute!* In the end, the researchers found this group was naturally inclined to read fast. They had a gift for it.[2]

Leadership gurus used to preach, "Find your weaknesses and improve them." The problem with this approach is, if you're not good at math, you're probably never going to get very good at math no matter what you do. And you'll end up frustrated.

Along the same lines, if you're a natural athlete and train yourself, you're going to get much faster and stronger because you're genetically inclined to do it.

It's the same with everything else in life. If you're good at something, you have the ability to rapidly advance in that area and get even better. But your weaknesses are what they are, and they're not likely to improve a whole lot.

At gallupstrengthcenter.com there is a StrengthsFinder self-assessment that costs around ten dollars. The results are a profile identifying your five greatest strengths plus action points and guides for understanding the results.

Dr. Donald Clifton created the StrengthsFinder test based on his lifelong research. It advocates for building your strengths rather than focusing on your weaknesses. StrengthsFinder has distilled the theory into practice by interviewing 1.7 million professionals from varying fields, quantifying the "personal themes" of the subjects, and coming up with thirty-four distinct attributes.[3]

My StrengthsFinder profile identified my strongest areas as:

- **WOO** (winning others over) – I have the ability to win people over to my side of an argument or discussion, and they will still like me.

- **Learner** – I'm going to study things that interest me, even if they're not related to each other. I'm naturally curious and want to learn.

- **Communicator** – I can tell you what I learned in a way that makes sense.

- **Futuristic** – I'm a forward thinker. I'm also a bit of a daydreamer, looking forward to future possibilities.

- **Arranger** – I love to help put people in places where they will do really well.

Those strengths certainly fit my role as a stewardship pastor with a worldwide apostolic calling. I guess God knew what He was doing when He gave me those abilities.

Another tool for discovering your gifts is the DiSC personality profile (thediscpersonalitytest.com). This test can help you learn how you are wired. It focuses on your personality, not your strengths. DiSC stands for:

- **D**ominance or **D**rive, which relates to the emphasis a person places on accomplishing results and the bottom line. These people are often assertive and may like to have power and be in control.

- Influence **or** Inducement, which relates to the emphasis a person puts on influencing others and building relationships. These individuals are often good in social situations and effective communicators.

- Submission or Steadiness, which relate a person's emphasis on cooperation, sincerity, and dependability. These individuals are often patient, persistent, and thoughtful.

- Compliance, Caution, or Conscientiousness, which relates to the emphasis a person places on quality, accuracy, and competency. They also tend to like structure and organization.[4]

If you can figure out how you're wired, you can gravitate toward your strengths. This knowledge is life-giving. It means you can rapidly move forward in your development without getting frustrated trying to work on your weaknesses, which at best will improve only marginally.

If you're a leader and oversee staff, you can figure out their strengths and weaknesses too. Then you can tailor their jobs and roles so they can quickly develop their skill sets and advance as their strengths grow. When you do this, you end up with happy employees who are highly effective and efficient. And they're having a great time because they're working in their strength sets.

Unfortunately, most of us don't enjoy our work because we're not operating in our strengths. Near the end of high school, people start asking students, "What would you like to do when you graduate?" The answer usually is something along the lines of: "Be rich. Do whatever will make me a lot of money, maybe become a doctor." But that person hasn't considered his strengths. If he doesn't have empathy, doesn't like dealing with medicine, and doesn't really like the sight of blood, he'll end up in a place where he doesn't fit.

Or a person may follow in Dad's footprints. "He's a CPA, so I'll be a CPA," he says. But if that person is not naturally gifted in that area and hates numbers, school will become a grind.

Those who follow these typical routes in choosing a career then get out of college, and instead of doing something they really love, do something they've been trained to do because they or their parents have spent a lot of money on their education and they don't want to disappoint anyone.

They enter a career they don't really like, then get married and have kids, which brings on financial responsibilities. So they stay in the job they don't like and aren't wired for because they need the income. And though they may be proficient in their work, they're not excelling.

The next thing they know, they're forty years old and thinking, "I'm not happy in life." They come to Gateway or a church like it and sit under great teaching and realize, "Oh. I'm not happy because I'm doing something I'm not naturally wired for."

At Gateway, because we have a stewardship ministry, those individuals could come to me, and I'd start asking questions and working with them to figure out how they're gifted and wired. This would help us determine what they're supposed to be doing, and life would become a lot more fun for that person.

Gateway has over five thousand volunteers, and we use the StrengthsFinder test to uncover their gifts. Then we match them with the areas of service that best utilize their gifts. When these volunteers come to church, they have a lot of fun serving.

Another tool for learning your strengths and gifts, especially in your personal life, is *The Five Love Languages* assessment (5lovelanguages.com). This is a great marriage communication tool because it helps you to understand how you and your spouse give and receive love. Though it is especially helpful in marriage, understanding these five love languages can improve your interaction in any relationship.

Here are my love language scores:

Physical touch 10

Words of affirmation 8

Receiving gifts 5

Quality time 4

Acts of service 3

My wife's scores are about 180 degrees opposite from mine. If I try to communicate from my primary love language—physical touch—she may not receive the message I'm trying to send her because her primary love language is receiving gifts. If I don't realize that, I won't understand why she didn't see that I was trying to tell her I loved her. Then there will be tension between us, all because we didn't understand our unique love languages. If I had brought her a gift, that would have spoken volumes to her.

When Missy and I put our StrengthsFinder, DiSC, and Love Language scores together, we found our arguments were in areas where our strengths didn't line up. For example, her number one strength is according to StrengthsFinder is belief, which means she has certain fixed core values that define her purpose in life. When my number one strength, winning others over, collides with her number one, she feels like I'm trying to talk her into something she doesn't want to do, and I feel like she's being stubborn.

When I bring her a gift, I think she's going to feel I'm buttering her up. But she actually thinks I'm wonderful because her number one love language is receiving gifts. Mine is physical touch. But if I approach her with physical touch, it can lead to miscommunication.

Again, this works similarly in other types of relationships. Our StrengthsFinder, DiSC profile, and Love Language results can also help us discover why things didn't work out on the job or at home as smoothly as we thought they would.

## WAIT FOR GOD'S TIMING

Understanding timing is the third key in discovering your calling in life stewardship. If we get all the other areas right but miss the right timing, we can make a mess. The Bible is full of great examples of the importance of timing.

When Joseph was a youth, he had a vision of his older siblings bowing down to him (Gen. 37). And when he was in his thirties that dream became a reality; he became Pharaoh's second-in-command. But I doubt Joseph would have planned the path he took to get there. In his immaturity, Joseph bragged about his dream to his family. That angered his older brothers, and they conspired to sell him into slavery. He eventually became Potiphar's assistant, only to be falsely accused of sexual assault, which landed him in prison. But then a high-pressure dream interpretation led to his promotion. In God's timing, Joseph ended up exactly where he was supposed to be. But God couldn't promote Joseph until he had matured.

Moses is another example of God's timing at work. When he was a young man, Moses burned with a desire to free his people. But when he killed an Egyptian while defending a fellow Israelite, Moses had to flee from Egypt, where his people were in bondage. Even though Moses was in trouble for standing up for an Israelite, no one was willing to follow him into the wilderness back then. In fact, one Israelite said, "Who made you a prince and a judge over us? Do you intend to kill me as you killed the Egyptian?" (Exod. 2:14).

Fast forward forty years. Moses is working with his father-in-law tending sheep. Then one day while he was out in the desert with the sheep, Moses encountered God in a burning bush. The encounter would forever change Moses's life, not just because he spoke to the living God, but because God set him on a new course. God instructed him to return to Egypt to free the people he tried to defend all those years ago. Now the time was right. And God delivered the Israelites in a miraculous way. (See Exodus 1–12.)

We can't dismiss the importance of timing. You can have all the passion and skills you need, but your plans will succeed only in God's timing. Even Jesus had to wait for His Father's timing. Look at what Jesus said just before He performed His first recorded miracle:

> And when they ran out of wine, the mother of Jesus said to Him, "They have no wine." Jesus said to her, "Woman, what does your concern have to do with Me? My hour has not yet come."
> —John 2:3–4

Even today, Jesus is waiting for God's timing. Someday Jesus will be back to rule on earth. But because of God's love and great mercy for those who don't know Him, the time for Jesus's return has not yet come.

Timing is critical in life. When Missy and I lived in Florida, I wanted to be on the staff at my small church more than anything. I volunteered; I served; I made myself available in any way I could. But I didn't join the staff because it was not God's plan. He used that time to train and prepare me.

Around the same time, God was launching a church in

Southlake, Texas, through Pastor Robert Morris that would fit me like a glove. I needed time to develop and so did Gateway Church. When the time was right, He brought us together.

As a wise pastor once said, "If you're going to miss God's timing, it's always better to be behind Him than ahead of Him." I'm glad I didn't miss God's timing, but I'm even happier that I didn't get ahead of Him.

## WHILE YOU'RE WAITING

Once we know our identity in Christ, our gifts, and the importance of waiting on God's timing, what do we do next? This is when we prepare for the intersection of life opportunities—that time when we hear God's call and recognize the part we are to play.

If you haven't figured it out by now, getting our finances in order is only a means to an end. It frees us to make life changes when God calls. We become open and free to respond to what God has prepared for us.

None of us can see our lives from the beginning to the end. We don't know what opportunities are in the future—tomorrow, next year, or twenty years from now. But until we hear God call, we are not to idly wait. We are to prepare. We must get ourselves in position to respond to God's call. We don't want to be like those in the Bible who wanted to first go bury their dead or check out their new oxen before following Jesus (Luke 9:59–62). We prepare so we can move when God tells us to.

How do we prepare? The Bible says, "Your word is a lamp to my feet, and a light to my path" (Ps. 119:105). This doesn't say the Word is a high beam or a spotlight; it's a lamp. When we walk with a lamp in the darkness, we really only see what's right in front of us. So, again, how do we begin to prepare for the opportunities God has for us?

I often encourage people to take personal retreat days when waiting for God to show them what He wants them to do next. This is like taking a sabbatical. Periodically, take some time by yourself. It can be an afternoon, a full day, or even a week. But take at least one afternoon a month to get alone with God. Every member of our ministry team participates in this practice. It has proven to be very effective, not only for the individual staff members but also for the ministry team as a whole as well as the congregation.

When you go on your personal retreat, grab your Bible and journal or notebook. Turn off your cell phone or leave it at home. You want to get rid of all possible distractions. Find someplace quiet like a park or a beach, or maybe drive to a secluded spot and sit in your car. You want a place where it's just you and God so you can ask the Lord: "What are You doing in my life right now? Am I being prepared for something? What are You saying to me? Are You speaking change or are You speaking, 'Stay steady'?" As you pray and read the Word, write down what you hear the Lord say.

When I take my personal retreat day, I pray about my relationship with Him. I ask Him, "Lord, how am I doing? Is there something in my heart I need to change? Are You speaking to me but I haven't caught it yet?" He usually has a few things to say to me too. And He's grateful for our undivided attention.

I also pray about my family, both immediate and extended. God will frequently give me insight into one of my family members, showing me things they're going through that I didn't see. And I pray for the church and the stewardship ministry. Almost every new initiative of the stewardship team at Gateway has come out of someone's personal retreat time.

You can apply this practice to your business as well. The founder of ServiceMaster, a group of companies—including Merry Maids, Terminix, and TruGreen—that provide a variety of services to individuals and businesses, told the Lord he would turn everything over to Him. He wrote in his auto-biography: "I don't intend to sit back and expect You to run everything, but I want You to tell me how to run things and send my way the men I will need to do the job.... I choose to serve the Lord, but You will have to show me how."[5]

Why not turn to God about your business, ministry, or calling? He's the ruler of the world, whose eyes roam to and fro, seeking who is faithful (2 Chron. 16:9). If anyone has the answers you seek, He does.

I also pray about my leadership, asking where I need to grow and change. I ask: "Am I efficient? What technologies should I be using? What do You want me to do with my schedule and upcoming opportunities so my time and talents best serve You, my church, my team, and my family? What do I need to know about my team members? How can I help them grow and prepare for the next steps You have for them? Are there ideas You want me to bring to my church leadership?"

I have ADD and am easily distracted. If *I* can stay capti-vated for a full day in this process, you probably can too.

I think my personal journey will help illustrate what this time of preparation can be like. When Missy and I ran the carpet cleaning business in Fort Worth, I knew God had called me to do that, but I had only a foggy idea of what His plan was. But He gave me certain steps to follow, and I learned I couldn't move forward if I failed to follow one of His steps.

First He told me to sell the business. That was frightening to even think about, but I did it. Next we moved back to Florida, near Missy's family, and I started the drywall construction business. As the business was growing, I knew He had more for me. "Lord," I prayed, "what do You want me to learn in this season of preparation?"

All He told me was, "Learn My Word."

So I listened to the Bible on audiocassette. As I mentioned previously, when I was working seventy hours per week, I heard the whole Bible in just one week. My favorite version was what I called the Darth Vader edition, read by James Earl Jones.

During that time I discovered a desire to learn more, to go deeper in my understanding of God's Word. I listened to the expositional version of the Bible, which explained the Scriptures verse by verse. I did this for five years—and I loved it! I knew I was being prepared for something, but I didn't know what. I only knew I did not want to miss the opportunity when it came by being unprepared in His Word.

While God was preparing me spiritually, He was also working on us financially, guiding us in the handling of our money with the clear message to get out of debt. God opened the door to full-time ministry as soon as we eliminated all debt.

Part of the preparation was learning how to operate in a ministry setting. I did a bunch of volunteer work and honed in on what God had gifted me to do—help people with their finances.

He sent me to The Hills Church, where I served as stewardship pastor for two years. It was a phenomenal experience. I was trained as the pastoral staff poured their love, experience, and knowledge into me. I was able to see how healthy church leadership functions together. While I was serving, I was also being trained for the next part of God's plan.

In His perfect timing, God opened the door to Gateway, where I need all that training and preparation on a daily basis and where I have the privilege to work with fantastic ministers stewarding an amazing move of God. I am soaking up all I possibly can from them.

I don't know what my future holds, but my heart's desire is to be a lifelong servant at Gateway Church. Here I believe I am using all my gifts and fulfilling my calling.

## THE SEASONS OF LIFE

The final piece of life stewardship is understanding the seasons of life. There is a concept out in the world called retirement. I think this is a disservice to people, even a lie. There is no model in Scripture for an unproductive time of life filled with relaxation. I believe God envisions us being always useful and doing things for Him right up until Jesus comes.

But the world's attitude seems to be, "I'll suffer through and when I retire, I'll do what I really want to do—what I really like to do." That's baloney.

I am all for retirement, but not as an end. It is a season during which we continue to live and serve. In that season we may initiate self-funded mission work. We can use our life-earned wisdom to mentor the next generation. Retirement is still a time to make a significant contribution to the kingdom.

Many people living to achieve their retirement goals never find their *today* goals. They miss years of today goals by focusing only on their retirement years. Psalm 92:14 is my favorite verse about retirement. It says, "Even in old age they will still produce fruit; they will remain vital and green" (NLT).

Our lives can be divided into three seasons.

**Youth**

- Childhood through college age

**Early Adulthood (Adult 1)**

- Marriage to empty nest

- Career

- Search for calling

- "Halftime"

## Golden Adulthood (Adult 2)

- Empty nest to glory
- "Retirement years"

## SEASONS OF LIFE

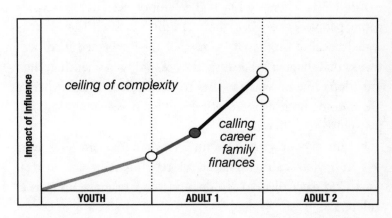

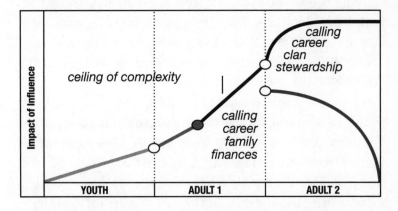

The first eighteen to twenty-two years is our youth. This is when we do the bulk of our learning. We're in school, and we don't have a lot of control.

Let's call the second season Adult 1. This is the first phase of adulthood. This usually lasts from when we get married until we become "empty nesters." We meet our spouse, launch our careers, and raise our families. This is also a time when we search for our calling. But the search can become muted as we get caught up in managing the day-to-day aspects of life. We find a place to serve that fits our lifestyle, but it may not be what God has called us to do.

Adult 2 is when we reach the "empty nest." This is when some people experience their "midlife crisis." They're frustrated because life hasn't been what they expected it to be. I think that happens because they're doing something their gifts don't line up with, so they're dissatisfied. This is where a life of doing nothing after retirement looks very tempting. Just play golf and chill out.

Let me encourage you. Adult 2 is when you can pour yourself into your calling instead of retiring. You can aim at what God has called you to do, and you can make an eternal difference.

Many people, when they reach sixty years old, are in their peak leadership time. With their experience and knowledge, they are hitting on all cylinders.

Our culture sees retirement as a time to slack off, and I believe that thinking does a disservice to the body of Christ. Retirement is when you are most useful, when people look up to you for who you are and what you bring to the body.

I think people should have their midlife crisis when they're in their teens because then they would be free to focus on what God has called them to do. They can live a life that never aims for retirement because they don't want to retire. They may leave their "job" or their "career," but they'll never stop working.

We all go through different seasons in life. Solomon said it this way:

There is a time for everything, and a season for every activity under the heavens: a time to be born and a time to die, a time to plant and a time to uproot, a time to kill and a time to heal, a time to tear down and a time to build, a time to weep and a time to laugh, a time to mourn and a time to dance, a time to scatter stones and a time to gather them, a time to embrace and a time to refrain from embracing, a time to search and a time to give up, a time to keep and a time to throw away, a time to tear and a time to mend, a time to be silent and a time to speak, a time to love and a time to hate, a time for war and a time for peace.

What do workers gain from their toil? I have seen the burden God has laid on the human race. He has made everything beautiful in its time. He has also set eternity in the human heart; yet no one can fathom what God has done from beginning to end. I know there is nothing better for people than to be happy and do good while they live. That each of them may eat and drink and find satisfaction in all their toil—this is the gift of God. I know everything God does will endure forever; nothing can be added to it and nothing taken from it.

—ECCLESIASTES 3:1–14, NIV

I think the idea of setting eternity in our hearts is why death seems so unnatural to us. We're not wired for death. We're wired for life. God created us to live forever.

Sin produced a short lifespan. Every time someone dies, no matter what the person's age, it always feels like a period in the middle of a sentence.

If I'm successful in teaching these concepts, you're going to aggressively pursue financial freedom so you can do whatever God has put on your heart.

Here's a formula for you:

1. Begin with your *identity*—who you are in Christ.

2. Add your *gifting*, which you discover by becoming a student of *you*.

3. Join them with *timing*—watch for God.

4. Add *preparation*—figure out how to discern God's voice and begin moving in the direction He calls you to.

5. Assess your *life season*—know what season you're in and plan accordingly.

This will lead to a powerful life of stewardship.

---

### Route 7 Road Map Step 6

1. Continue your strategic giving plan.

2. Pay off mortgage.

---

## YOUR ROUTE 7 ACTION PLAN

There's one area we've touched on in each chapter, sometimes hard, sometimes not-so-hard as the lesson required. That area is communication. As we near the end, I want to share an eight-point communication process that can be used in any area but is especially useful in handling money. My wife and I learned these lessons the hard way, and we hope you won't have to.

One of the keys to a successful life of stewardship is discussing and planning your finances with your spouse. As I mentioned earlier, money was once the worst area of our communication. Now it's our best. The communication process I'm going to share with you evolved over seventeen years of marriage. We have taught this many times in marriage classes, and we are proof it works.

**1. Remember that stewarding your finances is a team effort.**

When the paycheck comes in, Missy and I sit down with our spending plan, and together we give each dollar a place. It strengthens the marriage if both spouses know where the money is going. One spouse handling the money only creates tension and resentment. When a husband and wife work as a team, both know where the money is going, and this builds not only a firm financial foundation but also trust and unity in the marriage.

**2. Know the condition of your flocks.**

This applies to more than just the budget. Know where everything is in your finances. Being a bit geeky, I prepared a PowerPoint presentation that showed Missy where everything is. If something should happen to me while I'm traveling, she'll have all the information she needs to handle our financial matters.

**3. Follow the thirty dollar rule.**

Missy and I have an agreement not to spend more than thirty dollars on any one item without discussing it. If we find something we want to purchase, we call or text each other. It's not about asking permission; it's about staying accountable to each other and to our spending plan. I may find something I'd like to get. But when I talk with Missy, she may remind me of some expense or purchase I'd forgotten, and vice versa. This rule helps us to stay disciplined and on track.

**4. Periodically go on a vision retreat.**

Missy and I will sometimes take time away to talk about where we're going financially and in life. This is "us" time away from the kids and work. This is time when we press into the Lord together and share what He is speaking to each of us.

I mentioned at the beginning of this book that Missy asked

me if money were no object, what I would do with my life. I responded that I would teach what the Bible says about money. This happened on one of our vision retreats. I don't know if she would have asked it otherwise, but it allowed me to share my heart. When the opportunity came to serve as a steward-ship pastor, the job description matched exactly what we had outlined on that retreat. The retreat helped us to recognize the Lord's direction and/or confirmation when it came.

At least once a year, set aside time to discuss your goals and why you're doing the things you do. This will help you to stay in tune with each other. The retreat doesn't have to be expensive, though it makes for a special treat if you can afford something nice. It just has to be a place where you can get quiet and seek the Lord together. This will make an incredible impact on your relationship and your future.

### 5. Set long-term goals.

Set long-term goals and keep them in the forefront so they can determine today's spending decisions. As you know, our goal is to live on one-third of our income, give one-third, and save one-third. Getting to that point will take determination, discipline, and careful planning. Having a clear vision of where we want to be will help us stay on track.

Our long-term goals also guide us in setting short-term goals. For instance, we have a goal to live on a third of our income, save a third, and give a third, so our lifestyle choices are affected to reach this long-term goal. I like to ride my bicycle to work and I prefer to drive inexpensive cars. Could we buy more expensive cars and send our kids to private school? Sure, but that does not fit into our goals.

If you have kids, involve them in your goal setting. It will help them understand the basic principles of financial management and the decisions you and your spouse make. It helps them be a part of the process and take some ownership and responsibility for achieving the goals. It's awesome for them to see the outcomes you've discussed as a family. Goal-setting will strengthen your marriage because you and your spouse will be working together.

## 6. Husband, spoil your wife.

I'm not saying you should just buy her stuff, though that is part of it. I'm encouraging you to develop a certain kind of attitude about her. The Bible refers to it as honoring your wife. Do you hold the door for her? Do you thank her for the routine things she does for you and the kids? Honor isn't always grand gestures; it's also the little things. Ask yourself, "How do I treat my wife?"

Once, Missy was on a mission trip to India, and I decided to surprise her. We had planned to install wood floors. We budgeted and purchased the materials. We just hadn't decided when to install them. While she was away, I called the contractor and had it done. The challenge was hiding the ongoing mess in the house during her Skype calls to me and the kids, but we pulled it off. When I spoil my wife, she feels honored, and I set an example for my children.

## 7. Wife, adapt to your husband.

I enjoy bike riding—long-distance bike riding. Missy began biking with me. She'll tell you she's a girly girl. Biking in the Texas heat is just not her thing. But she does it, and it is a precious time for us to hang out and have fun together. She has even biked in some long-distance races with me and finished pretty well.

Biking also helped our marriage and finances. It gave her more insight into how I'm wired, and she could understand some of the things I might need for biking.

Finding activities to enjoy with your husband will strengthen your relationship and spending time together will improve your communication.

## 8. Husband, be gentle and create security.

The man sets the tone in the household. If I'm rattled or panicked about finances, or anything else for that matter, it can make Missy and the kids feel insecure. If Dad's losing it, there must be big trouble. If the man stays calm, the family stays calm.

It's like the story of the German sheepherder who lived in an area where NATO tank exercises were being held. When the canon was fired, the sheep would look at the shepherd. Because he stayed calm, so did the sheep. They took their cue from him.

The family is the same way. They will take their cue from the head. This is true in business and ministry as well.

Leaders, including the head of the home, must handle a lot of stress and pressure. But we don't have to feel like the weight of the world is on our shoulders. When stressors come at me, I turn around and hand them to the Lord. He is the one who creates the security by being our Father and Provider. Every worry is soothed as we release them to God in prayer.

Everything we've learned so far has been leading up to what we will explore next. Keep reading, and I'll tell you about the kinds of investments that yield eternal rewards.

## Chapter 9

# THE LAW OF ETERNAL REWARDS

ARTIN LUTHER IS often quoted as saying, "There are two days on my calendar—Today and That Day." The Bible commentator Matthew Henry wrote, "It ought to be the business of every day, to prepare for our last day."[1] Our eternal reward is the why behind all stewardship.

We can be really good with our money—keep our budget balanced, pay off our debt, and save a bunch. We can be living in the fullness of our calling. But if we've never really understand the law of rewards in Scripture, we'll miss out on opportunities to invest in eternity.

Everything we do in life leads up to one moment in our future. Everything we believe, everything we do, every decision we make—including our financial choices—leads up to our final review.

In school I dreaded reviews and tests. I didn't do well in a lot of subjects because I didn't pay attention and was easily distracted. I would come to class unprepared and pay the consequences, like having a 33 average in geometry one semester. If the subject interested me, I would do quite well. I aced government, history, and economics. When I knew what was expected of me and liked the topic, I had a totally positive attitude. I was ready and eager. But if the class was boring, my grades would definitely suffer.

God's review is nothing like the tests we took in school. He will give us the ultimate review. Imagine your whole life, from birth to death, laid out, each event marked and open to view. It will show the great things we accomplished and the seasons we endured. It will also show the opportunities we missed. The comfort is our sins won't be there because God doesn't remember them.

But everything we do on earth is on full display in heaven. Hebrews 12:1–2 describes a great crowd of witnesses in heaven watching us and cheering us on.

What we do with each day matters. James 4:14 tells us our life is like a vapor, a morning fog. It's here a little while, then it's gone. But what we do, every little thing, is recorded in heaven. It means something forever.

In this chapter I want to prepare you for the final review that will take place in heaven. We're going to examine several "Final Review Prep Questions." I'll list them here, and we'll go deeper into each one in the following pages.

- Will Jesus hold us accountable for the way we steward our lives? (The simple answer is, yes, He will.)

- Do our works result in salvation? (No, the Bible doesn't teach that we can earn our way to heaven with good works.)

- Can we earn and lose our rewards? (Yes and yes.)

- What is "treasure in heaven"? (We'll explore this in detail in the coming pages.)

- Can I change my eternal portfolio? Can I make a difference? Can I actually do something today that changes my whole eternity? (Yes, yes, and yes.)

- What happens after I die? (Keep reading; I will tell you.)

- Is heaven more than endless singing and fat babies on puffy clouds? (It sure is.)

As I mentioned before, when I was young, my parents were very involved in a small church. My mom was on the praise and worship team, and they sang a cappella style.

One day, on our way home from church, I asked her, "Mom, what's heaven gonna be like?"

She said, "It's going to be glorious, just endless praise and singing."

I didn't say anything to that, and after a while my mom asked, "Why the silence?"

"Well, crud," I said. "I don't like our singing. Are we gonna be able to do anything else in heaven?"

The idea of eternally singing every verse of "Amazing Grace" a cappella wasn't my idea of fun. My wife, on the other hand, would love to sing forever and forever. She has a beautiful voice and is gifted in that area. But I'm not wired that way.

Heaven will be more amazing than anything I can imagine. And I'm sure I won't mind singing along in worship of my King. But before we get to enjoy the splendor of heaven, we will stand for a final review before the judgment seat of God.

## Two Judgment Seats

There are two different judgments. We born-again Christians will face what is called in Greek the bema seat of judgment.

In 2 Corinthians 5:10 we read, "For we must all appear before the *judgment seat of Christ*, that each one may receive the things done in the body, according to what he has done, whether good or bad." (emphasis added). Romans 14:10–12 reinforces this:

"For we will all stand before the judgment seat of God. For it is written, 'As I live, says the LORD, every knee shall bow to me, and every tongue shall give praise to God.' So then each one of us will give an account of himself to God" (NAS).

Think of the bema seat as a raised dais with steps leading up to it. When Pilate judged Jesus, He was sitting on a bema seat.

In Scripture the bema seat is where Jesus will reward us and where we might possibly lose our rewards. Revelation 22:12 tells us, "Look, I am coming soon, bringing my reward with me to repay all people according to their deeds" (NLT).

This seat is different from the judgment most people think about. When most of us hear judgment, we think of the great white throne judgment as described in Revelation 20:11–15:

> Then I saw a great white throne and Him who sat upon it, from whose presence earth and heaven fled away, and no place was found for them. And I saw the dead, the great and the small, standing before the throne, and books were opened; and another book was opened, which is the book of life; and the dead were judged from the things which were written in the books, according to their deeds. And the sea gave up the dead which were in it, and death and Hades gave up the dead which were in them; and they were judged, every one of them according to their deeds. Then death and Hades were thrown into the lake of fire. This is the second death, the lake of fire. And if anyone's name was not found written in the book of life, he was thrown into the lake of fire.
>
> —NAS

The bema seat is for believers. The great white throne is not part of our future. We will see it, but those of us in Christ will immediately be with Him when we pass away.

God has the ultimate timeline for us. He knows the

destination of the saints because He can see the beginning to end all at the same time. We can't. God is like a person watching a parade from a rooftop or helicopter. He can see the whole thing. You and I are like a person watching the same parade from the sidewalk. From our vantage point, we can see only a few feet in either direction. Because we live in this time domain, our view is skewed. We can't see all that God sees.

How do we make sure our names are in the Lamb's Book of Life? It's as simple as John 3:16—by reading God's Word, believing it, and welcoming God into our life by receiving the gift of eternal life Jesus purchased when He died for our sins.

It's that simple. And it's also complicated because there are two types of faith, and sometimes we get them confused. I'll explain them to you.

## TWO TYPES OF FAITH

*Ascentia* is the mental acknowledgment of something's existence. The demons acknowledge and believe God exists. *Fiducia* is more than mental acknowledgment. It involves a trust in something, a giving over to it, a complete believing and acceptance of something. This is the kind of faith a Christian has in Christ.[2]

We exercise *fiducia* faith when we sit in a chair. We don't stand and ponder the chair for ten minutes. We don't pick it up and examine its structure. We don't push on the legs to make sure they're secure. We don't look for missing screws. No, we just sit down and expect the chair to hold us. A Christian has *fiducia* faith when he has real trust in Christ, a trust that is more than a simple acknowledgement that Jesus lived on earth at one time.

Another way to put it is this. There are many people in the world who believe Jesus existed. This is *ascentia* faith. But they do not believe He is their Savior—the one to be looked to and trusted for the forgiveness of their sin.

*Ascentia* does not lead to works that build treasure in heaven. *Fiducia* does.

*Ascentia* is not of the heart. *Fiducia* is.

Let me be very clear here. We are not saved by our good works. We are saved *to do good works.* The work of Jesus saved us. Our works, once we're saved, reward us.

## Treasures in Heaven

Jesus said in the Gospel of Matthew:

> Do not store up for yourselves treasures on earth, where moths and vermin destroy, and where thieves break in and steal. But store up for yourselves treasures in heaven, where moths and vermin do not destroy, and where thieves do not break in and steal. For where your treasure is, there your heart will be also.
>
> The eye is the lamp of the body. If your eyes are healthy, your whole body will be full of light. But if your eyes are unhealthy, your whole body will be full of darkness. If then the light within you is darkness, how great is that darkness!
>
> No one can serve two masters. Either you will hate the one and love the other, or you will be devoted to the one and despise the other. You cannot serve both God and money.
>
> —Matthew 6:19–24, niv

How do we build up our treasure in heaven? Paul tells us in 1 Timothy 6:18–19:

> Command them to do good, to be rich in good deeds, and to be generous and willing to share. In this way they will lay up treasure for themselves as a firm foundation

for the coming age, so that they may take hold of the life
that is truly life.

—NIV

Being rich in good deeds—being willing to share and help
others as God directs—is one of the ways we transfer our treasure into eternity.

In Matthew 19:21, Jesus told the rich young ruler: "If you
want to be perfect, go, sell your possessions and give to the
poor, and you will have treasure in heaven. Then come, follow
me." Jesus was talking about eternal investing. What we do
here bears fruit for us in heaven. Let's look at some of the reasons God rewards us.

## When we give up things for His sake, to be obedient to His call, God will reward us both here and in heaven.

And He rewards us generously. Matthew 19:29 says, "And
everyone who has left houses or brothers or sisters or father or
mother or children or farms for My name's sake, will receive
many times as much, and will inherit eternal life" (NAS).

## God rewards us for what we do (not what we believe).

Jesus said, "For the Son of Man will come in the glory of
His Father with His angels, and then He will reward each
according to his works" (Matt. 16:27).

## God rewards us for showing kindness to the undeserving, to those who are mean to us or who reject our gifts.

Jesus said, "But love your enemies, do good, and lend,
hoping for nothing in return; and your reward will be great,
and you will be sons of the Most High. For He is kind to the
unthankful and evil" (Luke 6:35).

Having a gift rejected is one of the most hurtful things we
can experience. God knows exactly how that feels. He gave
His only Son just to have Him rejected and crucified.

**God rewards us when we care for those in need, especially when we help meet physical needs.**

Mark 9:41 says, "For whoever gives you a cup of water to drink because of your name as followers of Christ, truly I say to you, he will not lose his reward" (NAS). When I get my wife a drink at the dinner table, I'm meeting her need and God recognizes this.

**God rewards us when we care for those too poor or incapacitated to pay us back.**

Jesus said: "When you give a luncheon or dinner, do not invite your friends or your brothers or your relatives or rich neighbors, otherwise they may also invite you in return and that will be your repayment. But when you give a reception, invite the poor, the crippled, the lame, the blind, and you will be blessed since they do not have the means to repay you; for you will be repaid at the resurrection of the righteous" (Luke 14:12–14, NAS).

This passage took on a whole new meaning for me after my family started supporting a ministry that works amid the poverty and devastation in Mumbai, India. Every time we volunteer or give to this ministry, I am reminded that though I don't always see how our efforts are benefiting the people of India, and they don't see us, God sees and He will honor our service.

**God rewards us when we are wise and productive in using the resources and opportunities He gives us.**

I don't know about you, but when I get to heaven, I long to hear God say, "Well done, good and faithful servant" (Matt. 25:20–21). In order to experience that, I know I must be a wise steward of the resources He gives me.

**He rewards us for being persecuted for Christ.**

Jesus told His disciples, "Blessed are you when men hate you, and when they exclude you, and revile you, and cast out your name as evil, for the Son of Man's sake. Rejoice in that day and leap for joy! For indeed your reward is great in heaven, for in like manner their fathers did to the prophets" (Luke 6:22–23).

Have you ever had someone attack you because of your faith in Christ, condemning your beliefs and calling you a liar? It's pretty frustrating because people like this can be hard to reason with. When it happened to me, it made me angry because not only was the person lying about me, he was attacking my God. I know I'm supposed to turn the other cheek. It's not always easy, but when I do, the result will be a reward in heaven.

**God rewards us for identifying with those suffering for Christ and for taking material loss.**

We read in the Book of Hebrews, "You suffered along with those in prison and joyfully accepted the confiscation of your property, because you knew that you yourselves had better and lasting possessions. So do not throw away your confidence; it will be richly rewarded" (Heb. 10:34–35). We must persevere in the midst of suffering because when we have done the will of God, we will receive what He has promised.

All over the world, our brothers and sisters in the Lord are being persecuted for their faith and martyred every day. By comparison, we have it easy here. Knowing how intensely fellow believers are suffering in other parts of the world has caused me to deepen my prayers for them.

Now that we've addressed what causes the Lord to reward us, let's look at what He gives us as rewards.

## ETERNAL CROWNS

The Apostle Paul wrote to the church at Corinth:

> Do you not know that those who run in a race all run, but one receives the prize? Run in such a way that you may obtain it. And everyone who competes for the prize is temperate in all things. Now they do it to obtain a perishable crown, but we for an imperishable crown.
>
> —1 CORINTHIANS 9:24–25

What are these crowns awaiting us in heaven? Here are five I've been able to identify.

### 1. The crown of righteousness

This is for those who believe Jesus will return one day.

> And now the prize awaits me—the crown of righteousness, which the Lord, the righteous Judge, will give me on the day of his return. And the prize is not just for me but for all who look forward to his appearing.
>
> —2 TIMOTHY 4:8, NLT

### 2. The crown of glory

This crown is for those who feed the flock and who volunteer in the church, serving and meeting the needs of the faithful.

> Care for the flock that God has entrusted to you. Watch over it willingly, not grudgingly—not for what you will get out of it but because you are eager to serve God. Don't lord it over the people assigned to your care, but lead them by your good example. And when the Good Shepherd appears, you will receive a crown of never-ending glory and honor.
>
> —1 PETER 5:2–4, NLT

### 3. The crown of life

This is reserved for those who have suffered for His sake.

> Don't be afraid of what you are about to suffer. The devil
> will throw some of you into prison to test you…If you
> remain faithful even when facing death, I will give you
> the crown of life.
>
> —Revelation 2:10, nlt

### 4. The crown of rejoicing

Soul winners and evangelists will receive this crown.

> For what is our hope, or joy, or crown of rejoicing? Is it
> not even you in the presence of our Lord Jesus Christ at
> His coming? For you are our glory and joy.
>
> —1 Thessalonians 2:19–20

### 5. The incorruptible crown

This crown will be given to those who remained steadfast
through persecution and trials.

> Everyone who competes in the games goes into strict
> training. They do it to get a crown that will not last, but
> we do it to get a crown that will last forever. Therefore
> I do not run like someone running aimlessly; I do not
> fight like a boxer beating the air. No, I strike a blow
> to my body and make it my slave so that after I have
> preached to others, I myself will not be disqualified for
> the prize.
>
> —1 Corinthians 9:25–27, niv

A crown that will last forever? I wonder what it will look
like. Actually, it's beyond our wildest imagination.

The Bible makes it clear that God will judge our works.
Again, I'm not talking about being saved by works. I'm talking
about the works we do after we accept Christ, both the good

and the bad. Some Christians will not hear, "Well done, good and faithful servant" (Matt. 25:21). There will be differing rewards when we get to heaven. We're not all going to receive the same crowns. We'll all be in heaven, but we'll have different rewards.

## THE JUDGMENT OF OUR WORKS

Some Christians will be ashamed when they meet Jesus. Surprised? The Bible says, "And now, dear children, continue in him so that when he appears we may be confident and unashamed before him at his coming" (1 John 2:28).

Our salvation is secure once we accept Christ. Even if we struggle with sin in our lives and die before we have fully changed our ways, we will not be cast away. The prodigal son wasn't rejected from his father's house. He just didn't have any rewards.

In heaven some Christians will "suffer loss." The Apostle Paul explains it this way.

> If anyone builds on this foundation using gold, silver, costly stones, wood, hay or straw, their work will be shown for what it is, because the Day will bring it to light. It will be revealed with fire, and the fire will test the quality of each person's work. If what has been built survives, the builder will receive a reward. If it is burned up, the builder will suffer loss but yet will be saved—even though only as one escaping through the flames.
> —1 CORINTHIANS 3:12–15, NIV

This passage says fire will test the quality of each person's work. If what we built survives, we will receive a reward. If it burns up, the builder will suffer loss but will be saved from the flames. The builder is still saved, but because he never quite made time for the Lord, he suffers a loss of rewards.

Although Christians will not stand before the great white throne judgment, at the bema judgment seat of Christ we will experience the consequences of the good we failed to do and the bad things we did. Paul wrote, "For we must all stand before Christ to be judged. We will each receive whatever we deserve for the good or evil we have done in this earthly body" (2 Cor. 5:10, NLT). And, "If you do what is wrong, you will be paid back for the wrong you have done. For God has no favorites" (Col. 3:25, NLT).

The good news is Jesus will wipe away all the tears in heaven—including the tears resulting from missed opportunities in this life.

We will not be judged for sin because of the work of eternal salvation. All sin—confessed and unconfessed—has been taken care of by the work of the cross. We will never stand against that sin at judgment. Scripture tells us, "For by that one offering he forever made perfect those who are being made holy" (Heb. 10:14, NLT).

Justification is a one-time thing, settled forever at the cross. Sanctification, on the other hand, is a moving target. We're continuing to grow and progress in our walk with Christ. This will never end until the day we die. We will never reach the point—in this life—where we can say, "I am completely sanctified." An attitude like that probably requires a humility test. We experience full sanctification when we die and go to heaven.

So, to quickly recap:

- Through Jesus, many are made righteous (Rom. 5:19).

- God forgives our sins and remembers them no more (Heb. 8:12).

- God does not remember our "sins and lawless deeds" and we no longer have to offer sacrifices for sin (Heb. 10:17–18). But this doesn't give us the liberty to live as heathens. We will lose our rewards if we do (1 Cor. 3:12–15).

- We live as free men and women, focused on the eternal gain that awaits us (2 Cor. 4:16–18).

## WHAT'S HEAVEN REALLY LIKE?

Have you ever daydreamed about what heaven is like? Do you ever wish you could have a peek? We can tell a few things about it by looking at Scripture.

**Heaven is an actual, physical place.**

Christ has traveled to and from it. So have angels, and in rare circumstances, people have traveled there prior to their deaths. See John 1:32, 6:33; Acts 1:2; Matthew 28:2; Revelation 10:1; 2 Kings 2:11; 2 Corinthians 12:2; and Revelation 11:12; 21:1–2.

**Heaven has light, water, trees, fruit, and animals.**

See Isaiah 11:6–7 and Revelation 6:2; 7:9; 17; 19:11; 21:23–25; and 22:1–2, 14. But even heaven is going to get a remodel. Revelation tells us there will be a new heaven and a new earth. We should be able to move back and forth between the two and bring things with us. The new earth will be different too. We can have fast bikes and cars with no worries about accidents or tickets (or running out of gas).

**Heaven is a city.**

See Hebrews 11:16; 12:22; 13:14; and Revelation 21:2. In heaven, the city's gates are always open, and people will travel in and out, with some bringing treasures into the city (Rev. 21:24–25; 22:14).

**In heaven we will worship God, serve Him, and rule with Him.**

See Revelation 5:11–13; 7:15; 22:5. We will have no doubts about what He wants us to do because we'll have face-to-face communication with Him.

**In heaven, we'll have rest from our earthly labors (Rev. 14:13).**

We'll be doing things in heaven, but those activities won't exhaust us.

**We will eat, drink, celebrate, and fellowship in heaven (Mark 14:25; Rev. 22:1–3; Luke 15:7; Matt. 8:11).**

Our resurrected bodies will be able to eat and drink. Jesus ate with the apostles on the beach after He rose from the dead. Abraham cooked and served a meal for angels who visited him, and they ate. We, too, will be able to eat, drink, and so on.

**There will be many dwellings in heaven.**

Jesus described heaven as having many rooms or dwellings—places He will prepare for us Himself (John 14:2–3). He knows everything we like, and our homes will be tailor-made for us. All we see on this earth will be in the new earth only in much, much better fashion.

Our imagination is the only thing that limits us in dreaming of what heaven will be like. We can have small groups and throw parties. We'll have a whole eternity during which to discover new things.

I imagine our entry into heaven will be like the last scene in the first *Star Wars* movie, where Luke, Leia, and Han Solo climb the podium to find a sea of people cheering and celebrating their arrival. We'll see family and friends who have gone before us. And we'll meet the people we've read about in Scripture. (This makes me cautious when I speak negatively about biblical characters. I may have to stand in front of someone like David and explain what I meant!)

Heaven is also the place where all our righteous acts—many of which were disregarded and even punished on earth—will finally be rewarded.

The prospect of what is waiting for me in heaven is what motivates me to move forward and get our finances in order. It motivates me to make wise decisions, to know my calling, and get in the financial position to pursue what God wants to do in my life. It drives me to be like the servant who was given five talents and earned five more. I don't want to be the like the servant who took his one talent and buried it.

I want to fulfill all that God has called me to be and do. Christian writer McNair Wilson is quoted as saying, "If you don't do you, God's creation goes unfinished."[3]

God didn't call me to be Billy Graham or Pastor Robert Morris of Gateway Church. When I stand in front of the bema judgment seat of Christ, He's going to ask, "Were you the Gunnar I called you to be?"

I want to be able to say with all my heart, "Yes." And then hear Him say, "Well done, good and faithful servant. Enter and receive your reward."

What about you?

### Route 7 Road Map Step 7

1. Practice extravagant generosity.
2. Live 100 percent strategically.

## YOUR ROUTE 7 ACTION PLAN

Can you imagine what the level of financial intentionality you will feel at the final stop on the Route 7 Road Map? If you are living in Step 7, congratulations! If you are still on the journey, keep going! You will make it! This is a lifelong journey for many people, but if we do not give up we will reach Step 7.

Keep yourself motivated by listing some of the things you'd like to do for the kingdom when you reach this stage of the generous life journey. After you've made your list, begin to include those things in your prayers each day. Thank God in advance for the opportunity to meet those goals. Even if you're still on Step 1 of the Route 7 Road Map, let this exercise begin to build your faith that you will one day live at Step 7.

# Chapter 10
# CREATING A CULTURE OF GENEROSITY

WOULD LOVE TO see pastors and church leaders all across the country apply the principles in this book in their own churches—but not just as a new program or curriculum tacked on to existing education efforts. If church leaders—and laity—really catch a vision for teaching stewardship and generosity, God may very well use them to spark a financial freedom revival in their congregations.

Imagine what your church would look like if the congregation was financially free. Dwell on that image. Think about the impact your financially free congregation could have on your community and on the world. Stewardship ministry is an integral part of making that happen.

The hope of the world isn't politics or economics. If the government could fix the economy, someone would have done so by now. The only hope of the world is Jesus Christ. He is the one who can transform people's lives. And the church, as the bride of Christ, is the vehicle God wants to use to bring that hope to the nations.

The church plays three vital roles in bringing the hope of Jesus Christ to the world.

First, we are like the *Mayo Clinic*. People show up at church hurting and don't know why. We diagnose the problem, help them get healed, and show them how to build a solid foundation on God Word.

Second, we're like the *Pentagon*. We've been given a global strategy and mission. We hear from our Commander-in-Chief in heaven, and we do what He tells us.

Finally, we're like *a military base*. We bring in the recruits—the believers—and we train and equip them. Then we send them out to shine the light of their freedom, including their financial freedom.

Our society is in a moral free-fall, but the Word of God is *solid* and living and active. We have to band together as Christians to work with God to reverse this course.

## Pastors Hurting Pastors

Early in this book, I mentioned that many church members have been hurt by improper teaching on stewardship and generosity. But this hurt has also been inflicted on pastors and church leaders. There are many walking wounded in pastoral ministry because other ministers abused and misused their gifts and misconstrued what the Bible says about giving.

As a stewardship pastor and a representative of the stewardship ministry, I want to apologize. You've been wounded because well-meaning pastors were not trained properly. And because of the role you play in your churches, the damage can be even greater than among the congregation. Please allow me to pray for you.

> *Father, I know You've purposed each and every one of us to do something great in Your kingdom. Lord, I ask You to bring to mind past wounds and hurts we've experienced in the church world regarding finances. I pray You give us the strength to forgive and set aside the hurt, even if we think we've already done that. Holy Spirit, bring to light the things that arise in our hearts that cause us to flinch when the church talks about money.*

*Lord, I pray for my brothers and sisters in the pastorate, that they would have a revelation of what Your Word says about money. And, Lord, I pray Your healing grace will rest on those who read these words, and that we will completely clear the deck and start over, walking in unity and powerfully advancing Your kingdom. In Jesus's name, amen.*

## THE PASTOR'S PERSPECTIVE

I realize that being in pastoral ministry is tough work. Consider these statistics about how many pastors perceive ministry.

- Fifty-two percent of pastors and their spouses believe being in pastoral ministry is hazardous to their family's well-being and health.

- Fifty-six percent of pastors' wives say they have no close friends.

- Fifty-seven percent of ministers would leave the pastorate if they had somewhere else to go or some other vocation to fall back on.

- Seventy percent of pastors don't have any close friends.

- Ninety percent of pastors feel unqualified or poorly prepared for ministry. (I think we're always going to feel that way. The Holy Spirit is never going to let us get ahead of Him to the point where we say, "I've got it, Lord." He won't let us step out in our own pride to do God's work.)

- Ninety-four percent of pastors feel pressure to have a perfect family.

- Fifteen hundred pastors leave their ministries every month due to burnout, conflict, or moral failure.[1]

I believe pastors can help and support one another. We as pastors, associate pastors, and lay leaders can work together to change these numbers and guide our churches into new areas of spiritual, physical, and financial growth.

When a culture of stewardship and the spirit of generosity rise up in a church, things change. The church becomes stronger. Of course the enemy will attack to stop the church and the financial world from working together in ministry. He will try to sow strife and division. But God wants us as ministers to resist these attacks and advance His will for our churches.

## WHY A STEWARDSHIP MINISTRY?

You may be wondering why it's important to develop a stewardship ministry within the church. Well, first, because God wants His people to be good stewards of the resources He gives them. Stewardship is not something God wants *from* us; it's something He wants *for* us. This is why I teach this material and why I work to give people a solid understanding of who they are in Christ in the area of finances.

To do this successfully, our motives must be pure. It is the pursuit of the spirit of mammon to say, "If our church had more money, we would be successful." Congregations who do this are chasing unrighteous mammon and serve a counterfeit god.

God has never told anyone, "You need more money," or, "Your church needs more money, and when you get it, then you can do all I've called you to do." He has never made money a condition of success or a sign of holiness. Money is one of the tools He provides to carry out His work, but His work can be achieved without money by those whose hearts are open to serving Him.

Second, we must teach stewardship and generosity because it's biblical. If as a pastor I'm charged to teach the full wisdom of God, I'm definitely going to search what the Scriptures say about money to ensure I'm getting it right. There are 2,300 Bible verses about money, and seventeen of the thirty-eight parables Jesus taught are on money and possessions.

A lot of Christians are shocked to learn the Bible has so much to say about money. It's shocking to many non-Christians as well.

While on a trip recently, I was seated next to a well-dressed man who wore Buddhist jewelry. I asked him what he did for a living, and he told me he oversaw a large region for a car manufacturer. Then he asked me what I did for a living. (I was so glad he asked.)

I smiled and told him, "I'm an eternal investment broker." Then I explained that I'm a pastor who teaches what the Bible says about money.

I could tell by his expression he was thinking, "How can I get out of this conversation?" Fortunately he was blocked in the middle seat.

As I talked about the scriptures and parables that referred to money, he became fascinated. I quoted verses and shared principles I knew he would recognize from his business acumen. I shared the roles of God and Christ in our lives and finances.

I could tell he was interested, but I didn't realize how interested until he tracked me down at the car rental center. He wanted to exchange cards, and we made plans to stay in touch. You might be surprised how God will use stewardship ministry to reach those outside the church.

Developing a stewardship focus in a ministry doesn't happen overnight. When a church decides to teach people about money, it must first go through the exercise with its leadership team. They need to be prepared and understand God's plan in this area.

When I first started teaching churches how to build a stewardship ministry, they didn't have a heart for that kind of outreach. It wasn't a big deal to them in the early part of this century. It was added to the catalog of things the church offered. But it frequently got lost in all the other stuff the church did, especially if people had been wounded and resented teaching on money.

Then the economy shifted. Pastors came to me needing help. "Our budget's a mess," they said. "We have to lay off staff. Stewardship is going to raise money for us, right?" It wasn't that their questions were bad, but they had the wrong motivation.

Now that everyone has pretty much adapted to the new economic normal, which still is not great, the questions and attitudes are different. The atmosphere in churches is changing. It is dawning on church leaders that stewardship and generosity could really change lives. Now pastors ask, "How do we establish a stewardship ministry in our church? I think it will change lives." This excites me!

I believe now is the time for pastors and ministry teams to ask themselves, "What do we want for the people of our church?" There are seven things we want to see in the people of Gateway Church:

1. We want them to have *Christ-centered financial views*. We want Gateway people to wear the biblical principles of stewardship like a contact lens so they see everything through it.

2. We want them to be *generous in their tithes and offerings*. We unapologetically teach on giving because we know what it's going to do in their

lives. Money given to Gateway will result in souls in the kingdom.

3. We want our people to *experience margin*, to live in such a way they have money left over at the end of each pay period.

4. We want everyone to be *debt-free*. We teach and counsel them in how to develop a plan to get there. Being out of debt creates margin and gives emotional, psychological, *and* financial freedom.

5. We want them to be *savers*. The Bible says we're fools if we don't save. We don't want a bunch of fools around our church. We teach the principles of saving for the short-, medium- and long-term. We want the congregation to save because we have fun when we're saving and seeing the margin increase. We save in order to be givers in every area of life.

6. We want them to live on a *spending plan*, assigning every dollar a task.

7. Finally, we want them to be *life stewards*, operating in their strengths and gifts. Once I met with an accountant who didn't like what he did. He wasn't detailed-oriented. Although he had created a successful practice over the years, running numbers had never been his passion. He went into accounting because his father and brother were in the profession, and it had become a family tradition. But he wasn't wired by God to be an accountant.

    I'm a strong advocate of personality

assessments and often recommend people take the StrengthsFinder assessment, the DiSC profile, and TTI Success Indicators. My accountant friend took these assessments and learned he was *not* wired to crunch numbers all day long. He shifted his responsibilities in his business and started doing things he was more suited to do, and it removed the burden he was carrying to be the chief numbers guru. Now he has tailored his role in his business to match his natural strengths.

At Gateway we believe everyone is a life steward. God has given them talents. My job as the stewardship pastor is to help our people identify these gifts and then get planted in the areas that will best utilize their strengths.

Another reason to teach biblical financial principles is this: Stewardship is not something we do, it is who we are. God created us to be stewards.

In Genesis 1:1 we see that God owns everything. The Bible says, "In the beginning, God created the heavens and the earth." That means He's the creator/owner. About twenty-five verses later, we find that He created us to be stewards.

> Then God said, "Let Us make man in Our image, according to Our likeness; let them have dominion over the fish of the sea, over the birds of the air, and over the cattle, over all the earth and over every creeping thing that creeps on the earth."
> —Genesis 1:26

To be a good steward is an integral part of our purpose on this planet. The Apostle Paul gives a nice summary of why we should teach generosity and stewardship in 1 Timothy. As I mentioned previously, at the time Paul wrote this letter, Timothy was a young pastor in Ephesus, a major trade city. He probably had the full range of socioeconomic conditions in his congregation. In these verses Paul gives insight into what to teach the people about money.

> Command those who are rich in this present age not to be haughty, nor to trust in uncertain riches but in the living God, who gives us richly all things to enjoy. Let them do good, that they be rich in good works, ready to give, willing to share, storing up for themselves a good foundation for the time to come, that they may lay hold on eternal life.
>
> —1 TIMOTHY 6:17–19

This is what we want for all Gateway people. We want them to use this passage as a model for their lives. That's why we teach stewardship.

## WE WILL BE HELD ACCOUNTABLE

I have just one final reason to give for teaching stewardship: At the end of time, we as pastors and church leaders will be held accountable. I don't say this to scare anyone but as a reminder of the seriousness of the call to ministry. When we have a deadline, we tend to work more diligently.

The Bible tells us, "For we must all appear before the judgment seat of Christ, so that each one may be recompensed for his deeds in the body, according to what he has done, whether good or bad" (2 Cor. 5:10, NAS).

At the end of the day, I am responsible for what I share and teach. I have the opportunity to train folks at Gateway. I'm also able to travel around the United States and to foreign countries to raise up leaders in this ministry. I am responsible for what I teach. But when you're called to stewardship ministry, you gladly accept it and do the best you can.

In Revelation 2 and 3, Jesus writes letters to seven churches and He uses a phrase that should make all church leaders pay attention. He says, "I know your deeds." He knows what is going on in each of our churches, and we will be held accountable for what we teach and don't teach our congregations.

## Getting It Done

I hope you see the importance of teaching financial stewardship in churches. Now, let me share how we get this done at Gateway Church. We're not simply building a curriculum; we're building a structure for this ministry that the curriculum flows in and out of.

I've been asked, "Are you a Dave Ramsey church, a Compass church, or a Crown Ministries church?" We are a Jesus church. Crown Ministries, Compass, and Dave Ramsey have excellent material that we have greatly benefited from. I love the leaders in all those organizations, but as a pastor, I and the leaders at Gateway Church are called to teach the whole counsel of God, not just a specific curriculum.

At Gateway, we divided the congregation into four groups. You may recall them from chapter 1. We use these terms to make sure we're offering something for everyone. Building a culture of stewardship and generosity in a church requires that all four of these groups are reached.

The first group is those who are *Struggling*. These families are not making ends meet. At one point, we were receiving eleven hundred phone calls per month from people who were hurting financially.

The second group is made up of those who are *Stable*. They have regular income but many times are one missed paycheck away from disaster.

Group three are those who are *Solid*. They are doing well financially. They're not wealthy, but they are managing their finances and building margin. The Stable and Solid groups make up 70 percent of most churches.

The last group is the *Surplussed*. These families and individuals have wealth and a high capacity to build more. They need to be ministered to differently—and our aim must never be to get something from them. God gave them gifts of leadership and generosity as well as the gift of building big things for the kingdom. Sadly most churches have abused them for their gifts, financial and otherwise.

Most churches fall off the rails by focusing primarily on the *Struggling*: "They're coming to our church, and we need to do something to help them." Or the church goes to another extreme: "We need to build some buildings, so let's minister to the *Surplussed*." Yet the majority of church members are in the *Stable* and *Solid* groups.

At Gateway, we've learned to be careful about what we do and how we do it. We make sure we offer ministry to everyone, in ways that best meet their specific needs. Let me explain how we minister to each of these four groups.

## THE STRUGGLING

The key to ministering to this group is *relationship*. We don't want our stewardship ministry to be seen only as the ministry people go to when they're hurting. When we give benevolence, we try to determine if the family is looking to have their immediate needs met or if they are looking for a life change. If they want life change, we will use our resources to help them walk through that process. If they seem to be in perpetual need, we will work with them to get them on the path to life change.

We have an exciting car donation ministry. We've given away

as many as seventy cars in a year. We sell the donated junk cars to pay for repairs on the better cars. This program has cost the church very little. It actually supports itself.

Not all our donation vehicles are cars we give away. In 2008, we received a Lamborghini with 2,800 miles on it. I told the church member we would accept it on two conditions. The first was he had to have lunch with me (I wanted to figure out what makes someone who gives away a Lamborghini tick; that is an emotional gift for a man). The second condition was we had to test drive the car together (which was incredible!).

We've had other exotic cars donated, including a Ferrari and a Dodge Viper. The staff knows I have a soft spot for these cars, so I frequently get to "play" with them a little, including taking our senior pastor for a spin. We sell these cars through a high-line auction and designate the money to whatever area the donor desires.

We also help our Struggling by providing small groups for accountability and prayer. These close-knit groups really help facilitate the "life change" process. In addition, we have a job board where Gateway members who own businesses post openings in their companies. And we have career workshops to help people figure out what they're good at. All of these efforts are tailored to meet this group's specific needs.

## THE STABLE AND THE SOLID

It's sometimes hard to differentiate the Stable from the Solid, so much of what we offer is available to both groups. This includes generational classes that address the specific life season of the group. We use my Route 7 class, Dave Ramsey's Financial Peace University, and our version of the Financial Hope workshop, created by my friend Dave Briggs at Central Christian East Valley Church in Phoenix. Financial Hope is a seven-week process during which families receive thirty minutes of teaching then meet in small groups with counselors who walk them through the steps to change. Using the workshop model helps us logistically provide a group counseling service to help more people at one time.

We also have equipping classes on many different stewardship topics. These classes offer prayer and discipleship, and help participants develop a solid understanding of what the Bible says about money.

Thirty-one different topical classes are taught through our stewardship ministry. We bring in church members who know the topics, and we structure the classes to answer three questions:

- What do we want them to know?

- What biblical principles do we want them to believe?

- What do we want them to do with what they learn in the class?

The classes cover topics ranging from buying a car to buying a home to preparing your taxes. One class taught couponing. There was standing room only, as over one hundred people showed up! After class the teachers prayed for two hours for those hurting financially. Some of the best ministry we've ever had has been in our couponing classes.

We tie the stewardship ministry in with other Gateway ministries through small groups and internal staff training. After we had trained the children's ministry in this area, the youth leaders came back to us with a curriculum they designed to teach stewardship to the youth. They created a fantastic series!

Our marketplace ministry brings in church members with specific expertise to teach on various business topics. We are very clear that these meetings are not for them to sell their products or services. It is to share their expertise and mentor other business leaders and potential leaders. It would be crazy not to use the best business mentors in the church to help others.

## THE SURPLUSSED

Those who have wealth are frequently the least-pastored group in the church. At Gateway, we take these men and women on a Journey of Generosity through a ministry called Generous Giving. Check out the website generous giving.org for more details. This journey often gives them a deep confirmation of what God is doing in their hearts. Or it gives them a revelation of what God wants to do in their lives.

Through our iDisciple program, we give iPods preloaded with my favorite sermons from Gateway's Kingdom Advisors program and our Generous Giving conferences to our high-capacity families. We ask that they listen for two weeks, then I get together with them for lunch. The purpose is not to get money from them. My motive is to minister to them in ways they may not have ever experienced.

One way we've ministered to these wealthier families is through strategic mission trips. A few years ago, I took seven men to Israel, asking them to think about ways we could bless the Messianic body in that country. We had a blast mixing ministry with sightseeing, building relationships with each other and with the leaders of the Messianic community.

These seven men came up with the idea to start a foundation to train entrepreneurs. The foundation would provide nine months of training and mentoring to potential entrepreneurs who applied through their local church and were recommended by their pastor. At the end of the training, they would present their ideas to a "shark tank." If it was a good idea, the foundation would invest. The first class graduated in May 2013, and it was a fantastic success!

This happened because, under God's anointing and direction, I was able to bring those seven men together and challenge them to use their God-given gifts to figure out how to create commerce to bless the Messianic body. To see what we've done, go to israelfirstfruits.org. Again, we build these relationships with our wealthier members to disciple them, not to raise money.

## Getting Started in Your Church

So, let's say you're now convinced you want to develop a stewardship ministry in your church. What do you do next? Simply developing a stewardship curriculum will not create permanent change in the culture of a church. Church leaders build the culture. Here are four important keys for creating a culture of stewardship in a church.

**If you are an associate or lay minister, get the support of the senior pastor.**

This is most important. The senior pastor must passionately be behind the effort. He has to seriously buy in to the concept. It can't be something he pushes to the periphery of the church. Ask him, "What has the Lord put on your heart? What do you want to see financially for your church?" Get him fired up, and keep him fired up. It may help to bring him to one of our Generous Giving annual events here at Gateway so he can see a stewardship ministry in action.

**Teach and train the staff.**

Get the staff behind you. If you are not the senior pastor, be sure to get his blessing. The staff may be intimidated at first. Walk them through the seven points I listed earlier in this chapter that we want Gateway members to take away from our stewardship ministry. Show them how each point will benefit them as individuals and as church leaders. Help them develop the vision of a changed, dynamic, prosperous church.

**Identify and build your leadership team.**

Many stewardship pastors are lay ministers, not staff pastors. If that describes you, don't worry. The church staff will help you recruit the team for the stewardship ministry. They know the key people. Look at having two teams. One will be the launch team. They may not be a good fit for the long-term, but they possess the skills and enthusiasm for getting the ministry off the ground. The second will be your implementation team.

**Figure out your demographics.**

Determine who in your church is struggling, stable, solid, and surplussed. Again, if you're not part of the pastoral staff, the church leadership teams can help refine this. If your church has multiple campuses like Gateway does, think about tailoring the stewardship ministry to each campus because each is different socioeconomically and demographically. One of our campuses has a higher income level and more married couples than another campus, which has 60 percent single parents.

## MOBILIZING THE PROFESSIONALS IN THE PEWS

Financial professionals in a church are either the best volunteers or the absolute worst. The majority are the best, but the worst, few though they may be, have caused a wall to form between the church and the financial community.

Say you're a financial professional but you don't know your pastor well. You offer to help him start a stewardship ministry. The first thing your pastor may be thinking is, "You're in this to build your business."

If you're a financial professional who feels called to begin a stewardship ministry, take the time to get to know the pastor and to let him get to know you. Have heart-to-heart conversations where you share your heart for this area of ministry. Help him see the bigger picture. Remember, 70 percent of pastors don't have a close friend. That may well become one of your primary roles in the church.

Gateway has networked with a community of financial advisors since 2006. They're called Kingdom Advisors, and I know the people in this group very well. They all work in various areas of the financial services industry.

I wanted a way to help these professionals use their strengths to help people in the church. And I wanted them to be prepared to do this because serving the church is different from the demands of their day jobs.

In order to prepare these individuals to serve in ministry, Gateway Kingdom Advisors take a Catch the Vision leadership class in which the participants confirm they are members of the church and agree with our tenets and philosophies. After they complete that course, we then check their giving record. They know this up front. We want to know whether they're giving to the church, because where their treasure is, there their hearts will be also.

After this, we take them through a specially designed Advisor Journey of Generosity, where I share my heart and learn what God is doing in their lives. Finally, they have to go through the Kingdom Advisors qualification process and maintain adherence to the Kingdom Advisors standards. A few years ago, through the Kingdom Advisors renewal process, which includes some due diligence on our part, we found that one of our advisors had been given a lifetime ban from the Securities and Exchange Commission. Because of Kingdom Advisors, I learned the man had major ethical issues.

This program has been a tremendous support for our stewardship ministry. These advisors are able to share their counsel with our members, and with the training we give them, they do so from a biblical perspective.

The ideas I've shared in this chapter should help get you started in creating a stewardship ministry in your church. Our Gateway Connect Ministry can help you further as you seek to develop a stewardship ministry. The Connect Ministry exists to come alongside churches and work with their leadership teams to help shape their ministries and develop the structures necessary for implementing their goals and visions. For more information about Connect, visit http://connect.gatewaypeople.com /about-us or contact us at Connect@gatewaypeople.com.

Taking the generous life journey can transform your congregation into a beacon for God in a world that is lost and hurting and seeking answers—answers they won't find in the government or anywhere else in the secular world but only in God and His Word.

I pray this book has stimulated you to dig deeper into what the Bible says about stewardship and generosity. I hope my words have given you insights and encouragement into how these biblical concepts apply to your personal life and to your church. I am excited to see what God is going to do in your congregation. Perhaps He will use you to ignite an outpouring of generosity that transforms your community!

# CONCLUSION

IFE CAN BE hard and the challenges of personal money management don't make it any easier. I caution you to please give yourself and others grace as you grow in your knowledge of biblical financial stewardship. The God we serve is a loving, gracious, and generous God who is conforming us into the image of Christ through trials, tribulation, and even in the blessing of His gifts.

The key to success in anything we attempt, including financial stewardship, is to never give up. Despite setbacks and heartache, don't stop. You will find success in budgeting, saving, and paying off debt through perseverance and diligence. Don't allow the word *quit* in your vocabulary. Refuse to let it be an option. You are not called to perfection, only faithful stewardship.

If you are naturally gifted to manage money, the body of Christ needs you to stand up and lead. Pour yourself into the Scriptures and get equipped to teach, counsel, and disciple others. Submit to your local church authority, and use your Romans 12 gifts of leadership and administration to help your fellow brothers and sisters. The days are short, and people walk in all kinds of bondage that keeps them from fulfilling their calling. You may be the coach God has placed in their life to help find the path to financial freedom and walk fully in their calling.

At the end of the day, I frequently think about the fact that one hundred years from now, all of us who are alive today will likely be on the other side of life, celebrating victories and sharing stories of God's faithfulness. Life really is a temporary assignment that impacts eternity. But while we're on this earth, we have the privilege of continuing the story of the Book of Acts.

As you walk through this generous life journey, keep the end goal in mind. We all have a part to play as followers of Christ.

In conclusion, I will leave you with Jesus's final dialogue with His disciples.

> Then they gathered around him and asked him "Lord, are you at this time going to restore the kingdom to Israel?"
>
> He said to them: "It is not for you to know the times or dates the Father has set by his own authority. But you will receive power when the Holy Spirit comes on you; and you will be my witnesses in Jerusalem, and in all Judea and Samaria, and to the ends of the earth." After he said this, he was taken up before their very eyes, and a cloud hid him from their sight.
>
> They were looking intently up into the sky as he was going, when suddenly two men dressed in white stood beside them. "Men of Galilee," they said, "why do you stand here looking into the sky? This same Jesus, who has been taken from you into heaven, will come back in the same way you have seen him go into heaven."
>
> —ACTS 1:6–11

To echo the words of my Lord Jesus and the angels who followed, "Go in the power of the Holy Spirit." What are you doing standing there looking at the sky? Get a move on, stewards!

# NOTES

## Chapter 3
### Five Stewardship Principles

1. "The Top Ten Causes of Death," World Health Organization, accessed July 6, 2015, http://www.who.int/mediacentre/factsheets /fs310/en/index2.html.

## Chapter 5
### Develop a Spending Plan

1. KBB.com Editors, "Average Length of U.S. Vehicle Ownership Hit an All-Time High," Kelly Blue Book, February 23, 2012, accessed September 17, 2015, http://www.kbb.com/car-news/all-the-latest/average -length-of-us-vehicle-ownership-hit-an-all_time-high/2000007854/; Brad Tuttle, "Driver Consensus: It's Silly to Upgrade Cars Every Couple of Years," Time.com, July 27, 2012, accessed September 17, 2015, http:// business.time.com/2012/07/27/driver-consensus-its-silly-to -upgrade-cars-every-couple-of-years/.

## Chapter 6
### Building Up Storehouse Savings

1. Ishaan Tharor, "Chart: If the World Were 100 People," *Washington Post*, January 6, 2015, accessed September 17, 2015, https:// www.washingtonpost.com/blogs/worldviews/wp/2015/01/06/chart-if -the-world-were-100-people/.

2. Scott Neuman, "Oxfam: World's Richest 1 Percent Control Half of Global Wealth," NPR.org, January 20, 2014, accessed September 17, 2015, http://www.npr.org/sections/thetwo-way/2014/01/20/264241052 /oxfam-worlds-richest-1-percent-control-half-of-global-wealth.

3. Hannah Wickford, "Typical Percentages for Household Budgets," TheNest.com, accessed September 17, 2015, http://budgeting.thenest .com/typical-percentages-household-budgets-3299.html.

4. Kathleen Hendrix, "Going Her Way: As Mother Teresa Prepares to Step Down, Critics and Supporters Assess Her Single-Minded Vision," *Los Angeles Times*, May 13, 1990, accessed September 17, 2015, http://articles.latimes.com/1990-05-13/news/vw-473_1_mother -teresa.

5. Robert Morris, "Breaking the Spirit of Mammon," Gateway Church, accessed September 17, 2015, http://gatewaypeople.com/sites /gwp/files/sermons/discussion_guides/breaking_the_spirit_of _mammon_02012015_discussion_guide.pdf.

6. Wikipedia, "Greed," accessed September 17, 2015, https:// en.wikipedia.org/wiki/Greed.

CHAPTER 7
A BIBLICAL VIEW OF DEBT

1. Baruch S. Davidson, "When Is the Next Jubilee?" www.chabad .org, accessed September 18, 2015, http://www.chabad.org/library /article_cdo/aid/513212/jewish/When-is-the-next-Jubilee-year.htm.

2. "Mortgage Definition," GrasptheWealth.com, accessed November 5, 2015, http://www.graspthewealth.com/news/words-mortgage -definition.

3. Liz Zuliani, "A Dozen Alarming Consumer Debt Statistics," EconomyWatch.com, May 21, 2011, accessed September 18, 2015, http://www.economywatch.com/economy-business-and-finance-news /a-dozen-alarming-consumer-debt-statistics.21-05.html.

4. Ibid.

5. Ibid.

6. TreasuryDirect.gov, "Historical Debt Outstanding—Annual 1950–1999," accessed September 21, 2015, https://www.treasurydirect .gov/govt/reports/pd/histdebt/histdebt_histo4.htm.

7. Lauren Carroll, "Rand Paul: Debt Doubled Under Bush, Tripled Under Obama," *Tampa Bay Times,* accessed September 21, 2015, http://www.politifact.com/truth-o-meter/statements/2015/apr/09/rand -paul/rand-paul-debt-has-tripled-bush-took-office/.

8. To see what a trillion dollars looks like, see "What Does One TRILLION Dollars Look Like?" at http://www.pagetutor.com/trillion /index.html.

9. "Average Interest Rates for Payday Loans," Payday Loans Online Resource, accessed November 5, 2015, paydayloansonlineresource.org /average-interest-rates-for-payday-loans.

10. Ron Liber, "The Most Serious Threat When Using Credit: You," *New York Times*, October 10, 2014," accessed September 21, 2015, http://www.nytimes.com/2014/10/11/your-money/the-slippery-plastic -slope-to-overspending.html?_r=0.

11. Tyler Metzger, "Study: Undergrads Relying on Credit at Record Levels," Creditcards.com, accessed September 21, 2015, http://www

.creditcards.com/credit-card-news/sallie-mae-study-undergraduate
-credit-card-1276.php.

12. CreditCards.com, "Credit Card Debt Statistics," accessed September 21, 2015, http://www.nasdaq.com/article/credit-card-debt
-statistics-cm393820.

13. Seema Mody and Giovanny Moreano, "As US Debt Grows, Here Are 23 Debt-Free Companies," CNBC, October 16, 2013, accessed August 3, 2015, http://www.cnbc.com/2013/10/16/as-the-us
-debt-grows-here-are-23-debt-free-companies.html.

14. Constance L. Hays, "J. C. Penny Sells Drugstore Chain for $4.5 Billion," *New York Times*, April 5, 2004, accessed September 22, 2015, http://www.nytimes.com/2004/04/06/business/jc-penney-sells-drug
store-chain-for-4.5-billion.html; Matt Krantz, "Companies With No Debt Fly High," *USA Today,* http://usatoday30.usatoday.com/money
/companies/2002-08-21-debt-free_x.htm.

15. Nolo.com, "Can my Student Loan Creditor Garnish my Wages?" accessed September 22, 2015, http://www.nolo.com/legal-encyclopedia
/can-my-student-loan-creditor-garnish-my-wages.html.

16. Justice.gov, "Census Bureau, IRS Data and Administrative Expenses Multipliers," Means Testing, accessed September 22, 2015, http://www.justice.gov/ust/means-testing.

## Chapter 8
### Life Stewardship

1. Peter F. Drucker, "Managing Oneself," *Harvard Business Review*, January 2005, accessed September 21, 2015, https://hbr.org/2005/01
/managing-oneself.

2. Donald O. Clifton and James K. Harter, "Investing in Strength," The Gallup Organization, accessed September 21, 2015, http://media
.gallup.com/documents/whitepaper--investinginstrengths.pdf.

3. GALLUP, "Lead With Your Strengths," Strengths Center, accessed September 22, 2015, https://www.gallupstrengthscenter.com/.

4. DiSC, accessed September 21, 2015, https://www.discprofile.com
/what-is-disc/overview/.

5. As quoted in Lake Lambert, *Spirituality, Inc: Religion in the American Workplace* (New York: New York University Press, 2009), 62–63.

6. Used with permission of Bob Shank, CEO of The Master's Program in Newport Beach, CA.

## CHAPTER 9
## THE LAW OF ETERNAL REWARDS

1. Matthew Henry, *The Miscellaneous Works of the Rev. Matthew Henry*...Volume 1 (London: Joseph Ogle Robinson, 1883), 464.

2. Matt Slick, "Are We Justified by Faith (Romans) or by Works (James)?" Christian Apologetics and Research Ministry, accessed September 21, 2015, https://carm.org/are-we-justified-faith-romans-or -works-james; see also Ligonier Ministries, "Faith Defined," accessed September 21, 2015, http://www.ligonier.org/learn/devotionals/faith -defined/.

3. Henry McLaughlin, "Over the Hill? Not Yet!" October 31, 2012, HenryMcLaughlin.org, accessed September 21, 2015, http://www.henry mclaughlin.org/over-the-hill-not-yet/.

## CHAPTER 10
## CREATING A CULTURE OF GENEROSITY)

1. PastorBurnout.com, "Burnout Statistics," accessed September 21, 2015, http://www.pastorburnout.com/pastor-burnout-statistics.html.

# ABOUT THE AUTHOR

I N 2002 GUNNAR Johnson, a construction worker, was
attending a Crown Financial Retreat in Florida. One morning
God told him He was going to use him in full-time ministry
to build stewardship ministries across the world in order to
set people spiritually and financially free to serve Him.

This book is a culmination of over ten years of faith, struggles, and obedience to carry out a very clear and precise vision
God gave him on how to build a stewardship ministry. It's
the story of how his encounter with God forever changed his
life course and taught him that how you handle finances is an
issue of the heart.

Johnson has served as the executive pastor of financial stewardship at Gateway Church in Southlake, Texas, since 2006. A
fan of cycling and an avid skateboarder, he has been happily
married to Missy, his high-school sweetheart, since June 1996.
They have three children—Faith, Katelyn, and Elijah—and
live in Trophy Club, Texas.

To learn more about starting a stewardship ministry in your
local church, visit http://connect.gatewaypeople.com/about-us.